OPPOSING
VIEWPOINTS®
SERIES

Mandatory Minimum Sentences

Other Books of Related Interest

Opposing Viewpoints Series

Black Lives Matter
Mass Incarceration
Race in America

At Issue Series

The Death Penalty
Minorities and the Law

Current Controversies Series

Drug Legalization
Police Training and Excessive Force
Racial Profiling

"Congress shall make no law … abridging the freedom of speech, or of the press."

First Amendment to the US Constitution

The basic foundation of our democracy is the First Amendment guarantee of freedom of expression. The Opposing Viewpoints series is dedicated to the concept of this basic freedom and the idea that it is more important to practice it than to enshrine it.

OPPOSING VIEWPOINTS® SERIES

Mandatory Minimum Sentences

H. Craig Erskine III, Book Editor

GREENHAVEN PUBLISHING

Published in 2019 by Greenhaven Publishing, LLC
353 3rd Avenue, Suite 255, New York, NY 10010

Articles in Greenhaven Publishing anthologies are often edited for length to meet page
requirements. In addition, original titles of these works are changed to clearly present
the main thesis and to explicitly indicate the author's opinion. Every effort is made to
ensure that Greenhaven Publishing accurately reflects the original intent of the authors.
Every effort has been made to trace the owners of the copyrighted material.

Cover image: RichLegg/E+/Getty Images

Cataloging-in-Publication Data

Names: Erskine, H. Craig, III, editor.
Title: Mandatory minimum sentences / edited by H. Craig Erskine III.
Description: New York : Greenhaven Publishing, 2019. | Series: Opposing viewpoints |
  Includes bibliographic references and index. | Audience: Grades 9–12.
Identifiers: LCCN ISBN 9781534502956 (library bound) | ISBN 9781534502963 (pbk.)
Subjects: LCSH: Mandatory sentences—United States. | Sentences (Criminal procedure)—
  United States.
Classification: LCC KF9685.M335 2019 | DDC 345.73/0772—dc23

Manufactured in the United States of America

Website: http://greenhavenpublishing.com

Contents

Chapter 1: Should Mandatory Minimum Sentencing Laws Be Reformed?

Chapter 2: Who Should Decide How Long a Mandatory Sentence Should Be?

Chapter 3: Do Mandatory Minimum Sentences Reflect Ethnic or Racial Bias?

Chapter 4: How Do Mandatory Minimum Sentences Impact the Crime Rate?

The Importance of Opposing Viewpoints

Perhaps every generation experiences a period in time in which the populace seems especially polarized, starkly divided on the important issues of the day and gravitating toward the far ends of the political spectrum and away from a consensus-facilitating middle ground. The world that today's students are growing up in and that they will soon enter into as active and engaged citizens is deeply fragmented in just this way. Issues relating to terrorism, immigration, women's rights, minority rights, race relations, health care, taxation, wealth and poverty, the environment, policing, military intervention, the proper role of government—in some ways, perennial issues that are freshly and uniquely urgent and vital with each new generation—are currently roiling the world.

If we are to foster a knowledgeable, responsible, active, and engaged citizenry among today's youth, we must provide them with the intellectual, interpretive, and critical-thinking tools and experience necessary to make sense of the world around them and of the all-important debates and arguments that inform it. After all, the outcome of these debates will in large measure determine the future course, prospects, and outcomes of the world and its peoples, particularly its youth. If they are to become successful members of society and productive and informed citizens, students need to learn how to evaluate the strengths and weaknesses of someone else's arguments, how to sift fact from opinion and fallacy, and how to test the relative merits and validity of their own opinions against the known facts and the best possible available information. The landmark series Opposing Viewpoints has been providing students with just such critical-thinking skills and exposure to the debates surrounding society's most urgent contemporary issues for many years, and it continues to serve this essential role with undiminished commitment, care, and rigor.

The key to the series' success in achieving its goal of sharpening students' critical-thinking and analytic skills resides in its title—

Opposing Viewpoints. In every intriguing, compelling, and engaging volume of this series, readers are presented with the widest possible spectrum of distinct viewpoints, expert opinions, and informed argumentation and commentary, supplied by some of today's leading academics, thinkers, analysts, politicians, policy makers, economists, activists, change agents, and advocates. Every opinion and argument anthologized here is presented objectively and accorded respect. There is no editorializing in any introductory text or in the arrangement and order of the pieces. No piece is included as a "straw man," an easy ideological target for cheap point-scoring. As wide and inclusive a range of viewpoints as possible is offered, with no privileging of one particular political ideology or cultural perspective over another. It is left to each individual reader to evaluate the relative merits of each argument— as he or she sees it, and with the use of ever-growing critical-thinking skills—and grapple with his or her own assumptions, beliefs, and perspectives to determine how convincing or successful any given argument is and how the reader's own stance on the issue may be modified or altered in response to it.

This process is facilitated and supported by volume, chapter, and selection introductions that provide readers with the essential context they need to begin engaging with the spotlighted issues, with the debates surrounding them, and with their own perhaps shifting or nascent opinions on them. In addition, guided reading and discussion questions encourage readers to determine the authors' point of view and purpose, interrogate and analyze the various arguments and their rhetoric and structure, evaluate the arguments' strengths and weaknesses, test their claims against available facts and evidence, judge the validity of the reasoning, and bring into clearer, sharper focus the reader's own beliefs and conclusions and how they may differ from or align with those in the collection or those of their classmates.

Research has shown that reading comprehension skills improve dramatically when students are provided with compelling, intriguing, and relevant "discussable" texts. The subject matter of these collections could not be more compelling, intriguing, or urgently relevant to today's students and the world they are poised to inherit. The anthologized articles and the reading and discussion questions that are included with them also provide the basis for stimulating, lively, and passionate classroom debates. Students who are compelled to anticipate objections to their own argument and identify the flaws in those of an opponent read more carefully, think more critically, and steep themselves in relevant context, facts, and information more thoroughly. In short, using discussable text of the kind provided by every single volume in the Opposing Viewpoints series encourages close reading, facilitates reading comprehension, fosters research, strengthens critical thinking, and greatly enlivens and energizes classroom discussion and participation. The entire learning process is deepened, extended, and strengthened.

For all of these reasons, Opposing Viewpoints continues to be exactly the right resource at exactly the right time—when we most need to provide readers with the critical-thinking tools and skills that will not only serve them well in school but also in their careers and their daily lives as decision-making family members, community members, and citizens. This series encourages respectful engagement with and analysis of opposing viewpoints and fosters a resulting increase in the strength and rigor of one's own opinions and stances. As such, it helps make readers "future ready," and that readiness will pay rich dividends for the readers themselves, for the citizenry, for our society, and for the world at large.

Introduction

> *"Since 2009, more than half the states have passed legislation to relax mandatory minimums and restore judicial discretion—including deep-red Georgia, Louisiana, Mississippi, Oklahoma, and South Carolina. A new crop of prosecutors is openly questioning the use of long prison terms for minor drug crimes. And a bill to ease federal sentencing has bipartisan support in Congress. [Attorney General Jeff] Sessions is bent on reversing this progress."*
>
> —*Nancy Gertner and Chiraag Bains,* Washington Post, *May 15, 2017*

Mandatory minimum sentences have their place in the judicial system. Designed to keep people who commit particularly heinous crimes off the street, or repeat offenders from committing the same crime over and over, or to act as a deterrent, they have been in place in many states for decades. But they are not without controversy. There are those who feel mandatory minimum sentences usurp a judge's ability to make a punishment fit the crime, at his or her discretion, after considering some mitigating facts. Some feel that mandatory minimum sentences are too harsh. Others feel they are discriminatory and lead to racial and ethnic disparities. Still others feel mandatory minimum sentences only cause prison overcrowding, putting excessive burdens on the taxpayer, the money being better spent on treatment and rehab programs. Others would prefer there be more alternative sentencing options available.

Some might suggest that mandatory minimum sentences have been around since ancient times, as in: "An eye for an eye, and a tooth for a tooth." In the United States, Congress passed the Boggs Act of 1951, making a first-time cannabis possession offense a minimum of two to ten years and a fine of up to $20,000. But, in 1970, mandatory penalties for cannabis offenses were repealed. New York State introduced mandatory minimum sentences of fifteen years to life for possession of more than 4 ounces (113 grams) of a hard drug in 1973. Congress enacted different mandatory minimum sentences for drugs (including marijuana) with passage of the Anti-Drug Abuse Act of 1986.

Demands for harsher and more definitive sentencing became extremely popular in the 1980s and 1990s. Mothers Against Drunk Driving (MADD) led a grassroots campaign in the early 1980s to successfully change laws nationwide to require mandatory jail time for impaired drivers. Reformers have demanded abolition of parole or additional controls such as notifying the community when a sex offender is released. These include Megan's Law and the Washington State Sexual Predator law. In addition to mandatory minimum sentencing laws for drunk driving and drug crimes, there are also laws pertaining to use of a firearm while committing a violent crime, mandatory registration as a sex offender (e.g., sexual assault and child pornography offenses), and certain financial crimes.

The Sentencing Reform Act (SRA) of 1984 created the federal sentencing guideline system. Before that, there was no appellate review of federal sentences. The SRA provided for significant appellate review of all guideline sentences. California enacted a "Three Strikes Law," which was the first mandatory sentencing law to gain widespread publicity in 1994. The law requires a minimum of twenty-five years of imprisonment after conviction of a third felony. Similar laws were adopted in most US jurisdictions.

Mandatory penalties are intended to eliminate judicial discretion in choosing among various punishment options, under the assumption that judges are too lenient and offenders are therefore neither generally deterred from crime nor specifically deterred because some are not incarcerated long enough to prevent their returning to crime. Mandatory sentencing laws require judges to sentence the convicted offender to a specific prison term of a fixed amount of time, but there is wide variation in how these laws are applied. A prosecutor's decision whether to charge a crime to which a mandatory sentence will attach varies depending on local prosecutorial charging policies and plea-bargaining practices, and the actual charge of conviction is flexible in a plea bargain. Mandatory sentences differ from determinative or guidelines sentences because they include no range of time within which a judge has discretion to set a sentence.

According to the US Sentencing Commission (USC), the average prison sentence for offenders convicted of an offense carrying a mandatory minimum penalty is 114 months, while the average prison sentence for offenders convicted of an offense not carrying a mandatory minimum penalty is 33 months. According to the USC, approximately one-quarter of all federal defendants are convicted of an offense that carries a mandatory minimum sentence such as drug-trafficking offenses, use of a firearm during a crime of violence or drug-trafficking offenses, or a felon's illegal possession of a firearm after having been convicted of three violent felonies or serious drug-trafficking offenses.

A sentencing court can impose a sentence below an otherwise applicable statutory mandatory minimum based on the defendant's "substantial assistance" to the prosecution in the investigation, or prosecution of another person, and in certain drug-trafficking cases, if the defendant qualifies for the statutory "Safety Valve" contained in USC section 3553(f). The Safety Valve statute was created in 1994 to reduce mandatory sentences for drug offenders and only applies in cases in which a defendant faces a mandatory minimum penalty after being convicted of certain types of drug-trafficking offenses. There are five criteria governing a court's decision as to whether a defendant qualifies for a safety valve; it typically applies only to lower-level, non-violent drug offenders.

According to a 2014 survey of federal district judges, most judges today find that the guidelines established by the USC in response to Congress's directives in the SRA in 1987 generally have increased certainty and fairness in meeting the purposes of punishment and have reduced unwarranted sentencing disparities. A majority of judges also favor the current guideline system over alternative systems. Today, groups and organizations such as Families Against Mandatory Minimums (FAMM), the American Bar Association, and the ACLU are calling for widespread repeal of the mandatory minimum sentencing laws. Yet US Attorney General Jeff Sessions is a supporter of mandatory minimum sentences, believing they are responsible for reduced crime rates.

With prisons at capacity, generations of broken families, and drugs still a scourge on society, the question arises whether mandatory minimum sentences are fair or even successful. In *Opposing Viewpoints: Mandatory Minimum Sentences*, authors approach the topic from a diverse array of perspectives in chapters titled "Should Mandatory Minimum Sentencing Laws Be Reformed?," "Who Should Decide How Long a Mandatory Sentence Should Be?," "Do Mandatory Minimum Sentences Reflect Ethnic or Racial Bias?," and "How Do Mandatory Minimum Sentences Impact the Crime Rate?" The divergent viewpoints on the subject illustrate the uncertainty of the efficacy of mandatory minimum sentences, as well as a strong desire by many to revise legal policies with the aim of creating a better, safer, and more equitable society.

OPPOSING
VIEWPOINTS®
SERIES

Should Mandatory Minimum Sentencing Laws Be Reformed?

Chapter Preface

Mandatory sentencing laws have been around since passage of the Boggs Act of 1951 and have been successful at deterring crime at some levels. The United States experienced a drop in crime when many of the mandatory sentencing laws were put into place in the 1980s. But a survey in 2014 showed that almost 80 percent of Americans supported the elimination of mandatory sentencing laws. How did the shift happen?

Some feel that mandatory minimums undermine a commitment to fairness and justice by preventing judges from considering the defendant's background and circumstances of the offense when determining the sentence. And that this leads to soaring prison populations, causing overcrowding and excessive costs to public taxpayers. According to the Pew Charitable Trusts: "Between 1980 and 2013, the federal imprisonment rate increased 518 percent, and spending on the federal prison system increased from $970 million to more than $6.7 billion."

Supporters of mandatory sentencing assert these laws achieve deterrence and incapacitation with more certainty than sentencing under other structures. They feel the elimination of judicial discretion is important in the endeavor of maintaining fairness in sentencing among criminals committing the same crime. They argue judges had nearly unlimited power in the sentencing of individuals before the use of mandatory minimum sentences. They also claim it serves as a deterrent to crime.

Opponents of mandatory minimum sentences say that mandatory sentences are ineffective in deterring crime, claiming it is more closely related to the certainty of apprehension rather than knowing the severity of the punishment. Many offenders will consider that the probability of getting caught is low and therefore worth taking the risk, despite the severity of the punishment. Supporters cite increased public safety. With longer mandatory minimum sentences, criminals can be kept off the streets and prosecutors hold leverage over the defendant, increasing the possibility of the defendant giving them cooperation in exchange for a reduced sentence.

Another point argued is that eliminating judicial discretion increased fairness in the criminal justice system. Opponents charge that fairness is, in fact, decreased with low-level criminals. By elimination of considering the circumstances of each crime, lower-level criminals face consequences similar to higher-level, dangerous defendants.

Also to be considered: Mandatory minimum sentencing shifts discretion from judges to the prosecutors who decide what charges to bring against the defendant. They can stack the deck by overcharging a defendant in order to get them to plead guilty. Opponents argue that it is the role of a judge and not the prosecutor to apply discretion given the facts of a case. In addition to fairness arguments, opponents think treatment is more cost-effective than long sentences. Since 2015, several organizational reformers have resolved to change the criminal justice system and reduce mandatory minimum sentencing laws.

> "*Mandatory minimum sentences have persisted for decades despite opposition by citizens and judges.*"

Mandatory Minimum Sentencing Laws Are Costly and Unjust

The Criminal Justice Policy Foundation

In the following viewpoint, the Criminal Justice Policy Foundation argues that mandatory minimum sentences have failed to address the problems they were enacted to solve. Designed to limit variances among judges, they have effectively created a system in which prosecutors use the laws as easy leverage in order to obtain plea deals, gaining the power that the judges have yielded. The sentences have resulted in an overcrowded prison system and a skyrocketing federal prison budget that could be spent on reform and other social programs. Although many lawmakers now agree that mandatory minimum sentences have not been effective, efforts to reform the laws have not gained traction. The Criminal Justice Policy Foundation educates the public about the impact of drug policy on the criminal justice system in the United States.

"Mandatory Minimums and Sentencing Reform," Criminal Justice Policy Foundation. Reprinted by permission.

As you read, consider the following questions:

1. In what year were federal mandatory minimum laws in drug cases enacted?
2. To whom do mandatory sentences transfer the power?
3. What was the federal prison budget in fiscal year 2017?

Mandatory minimum sentencing laws force a judge to hand down a minimum, often long, prison sentence based on a prosecutor's choice of charges brought against a defendant. Many states have such laws. These laws take away from a judge, when deciding on punishment, the traditional authority to account for the actual circumstances of the crime and the individual defendant. Federal mandatory minimum laws in drug cases, enacted in 1986, carry very long maximum sentences—5 years up to 40 years, and 10 years up to life imprisonment. These laws were enacted before the implementation in 1987 of the Sentencing Reform Act of 1984 which had been delayed by litigation and the development of the new sentencing guidelines. For over two decades, the sentencing guidelines also had a near-mandatory quality, and imposed long sentences for drug quantities greater than the minimum trigger quantities in the drug statute, 21 U.S.C.. 841(b)(1). The mandatory minimum drug laws and the sentencing guidelines have contributed to the federal prison system becoming the largest prison system in the United States.

Mandatory sentences have the effect of transferring sentencing power from judges to prosecutors. Prosecutors frequently threaten to bring charges carrying long mandatory minimum sentences and longer guidelines sentences to scare a defendant to plead guilty in exchange for a reduced sentence and give up every factual and legal basis for a defense. As a result, at least 95 percent of federal drug defendants plead guilty. CJPF is pleased to have worked with the team that produced the movie, Incarcerating US, to reform mandatory minimums, as well as allies such as FAMM—Families Against Mandatory Minimums.

As Assistant Counsel to the House Judiciary Committee from 1979 to 1989, CJPF Executive Director Eric E. Sterling helped the Members of Congress he served to write the federal mandatory minimum sentences for drug and gun crimes. He and CJPF now oppose mandatory minimum sentences because they are antithetical to achieving justice in individual cases. Cumulatively, they have been misused by the Department of Justice. Combined with sentencing guidelines, most of the sentences that have been imposed imposed by federal judges in the past 30 years are unjustly long for the conduct and culpability of the defendant. The justice system has been distorted by removing from judges the deciding of the proper sentence in a case, and substituting a matrix of quantities and other circumstances that can be shaped by the prosecutor's charging choices. The elimination of judicial discretion in sentencing has allowed prosecutors to acquire excessive power to impose sentences. Prosecutors threaten defendants who plan to assert a legal defense that they are failing to "take responsibility" and that they will work to increase the offense levels of the sentencing guidelines. On the other hand, prosecutors negotiate more generously with defendants who can reveal information about other defendants or the location of the hidden proceeds of the crimes. Higher-level offenders with greater knowledge of the details of a criminal organization have the power to manipulate the system by trading what they know for a shorter sentence in contrast to lower-level offenders who have no such knowledge.

Introduction

Mandatory minimum sentencing laws are statutes that require judges to sentence offenders to a specified minimum prison term for a specific crime. For example, a minimum 5-year sentence (up to 40 years) must be imposed for distribution of 5 grams of methamphetamine, only a 5-day supply for a heavy user (see a complete list of federal mandatory minimums here). Mandatory minimums for drug offenses are generally triggered by the weight of the drugs. The weights of every transaction carried out by a defendant, or conspiracy, are totaled. In addition, weights that are boasted about or admitted to are counted as well as weights of drugs actually purchased or seized. The report of a witness or informant, even if not under oath, and easily exaggerated, of some number of transactions, or the size of a sale or shipment, gets counted for determining the weight that can trigger a mandatory minimum or high-level sentencing guideline penalty.

Unlike the complementary system of sentencing guidelines, which now provide a suggested sentence range after a computation of circumstances by the judge (and from which the judge can further deviate or depart from in response to all the circumstances), mandatory minimum laws allow no room for judicial discretion. As a result, each year tens of thousands of low-level state and federal defendants face harsh punishments that are often denounced by the judges forced to impose them at the time of sentencing.

A Blunt Tool of the Drug War

Congress and the states have implemented mandatory minimums for a variety of offenses, but they are used especially frequently in drug cases. Federal drug cases usually involve more than one defendant and are often charged as conspiracies. In conspiracies, drug-related mandatory minimum punishments are based on the total weight of drugs of all the transactions all the persons who are part of the conspiracy are alleged to have carried out, and not on the individual defendant's actual level of involvement. Thus, a single-trip drug courier faces the same penalty as the ringleader who arranged all the shipments of the organization. Not only are the terms of imprisonment much too high, but Congress also set the drug weight thresholds too low to identify true high-level offenders that should be the target of federal investigation. For methamphetamine, offenders face a minimum five-year sentence for distribution of five grams, the weight of five Sweet-n-Low(R) packets, when a heavy user might go through a gram in a day. A genuine high-level trafficker arranges multiple shipments of hundreds of kilograms.

In addition, all the non-drug ingedients of a drug shipment are counted in the weight. 500 grams of 50% pure cocaine is counted as 500 grams of cocaine, not 250 grams. A dose of the psychedelic drug LSD might be 50 millionths of a gram—such a tiny amount, it needs to placed on some kind of carrier such as a small piece of paper which, as light as it is is, weighs much more. A sheet of paper weighs 4 or 5 grams. It could be divided into 100 doses of 50 micrograms each. The distribution of one gram of LSD carries a minimum sentence of 5 years. Therefore the possession with intent to distribute 100 doses of 50 micograms each on a sheet of paper triggers the mandatory minimum even though the total weight of the LSD is .005 grams.

Although Congress passed mandatory minimum laws in 1986 with the directive to the Justice Department to focus on "major drug traffickers," that has not been the case. In its most recent comprehensive study, the US Sentencing Commission reported in 2011 that "high-level" suppliers or importers made up only 10.9% of federal defendants, wholesalers of any amount—21.2%, street-level dealers—17.2%, and couriers—23% sentenced for drug offenses. Only 2.2% were managers or supervisors. The rest of federal drug defendants were other low-level offenders, even marginally-involved friends and family of the accused.

A Waste of Money

Excessively long sentences are not only unjust but extremely expensive and wasteful. In FY 2015, the average cost of incarceration of a federal prisoner was just under $32,000. The federal prison budget has risen from less than $3.7 billion in 2000 and less than $5 billion in 2006 to about $7 billion in 2017. This exceeds the $5.5 billion allocated by the federal government to care for all the homeless people in the US. (It was estimated that on a January night in 2014 there were more than half a million homeless people in America's shelters and streets.)

Prospects for Reform

Mandatory minimum sentences have persisted for decades despite opposition by citizens and judges. But over the last few years, South Carolina and Rhode Island have eliminated at least some drug mandatory minimums completely, presenting a model for federal reform. CJPF has been educating the public about the need for reform for decades. In the summer of 2015, Criminal Justice Policy Foundation Executive Director Eric E. Sterling called on President Obama to address mandatory minimums during his remaining months in office. While hopes were high for reform to pass in the 114th Congress, President Obama's advocacy was inadequate and no legislation was enacted before Congress adjourned in 2016.

On October 4, 2017, Senator Chuck Grassley, the Chair of the Senate Judiciary Committee, with 10 other Senators introduced a new sentencing reform bill, S.1917. Attorney General Jefferson B. Sessions, a career prosecutor before his election to the Senate, has been a prominent defender of mandatory minimum sentences. At the Department of Justice, he has brought into senior leadership others who share his view. Jared Kushner, son-in-law to President Donald Trump, has been meeting with Senators about sentencing reform. The position of the Administration at the end of 2017 on the new sentencing reform legislation has not been announced.

> *"Locking up offenders also incapacitates them for the term of their imprisonment and thereby protects the public."*

It Is Difficult to Predict the Impact of Mandatory Minimum Sentencing Reforms

Paul Larkin and Evan Bernick

In the following excerpted viewpoint, Paul Larkin and Evan Bernick argue that mandatory minimum sentences are the product of good intentions, but good intentions do not always make good policy. Good results are also necessary. Recognizing this fact, there are public officials on both sides of the aisle who support amending some components of federal mandatory minimum sentencing laws. But before such reform can proceed, Congress must ask itself: With respect to each crime, is justice best served by having legislatures assign fixed penalties to that crime? Or should legislatures leave judges more or less free to tailor sentences to the aggravating and mitigating facts of each criminal case within a defined range? Paul Larkin is a senior research fellow at The Heritage Foundation's Meese Center for Legal and Judicial Studies, Institute for Constitutional Government. Evan Bernick is a visiting fellow at the Meese Center.

"Reconsidering Mandatory Minimum Sentences: The Arguments for and Against Potential Reforms," by Paul Larkin and Evan Bernick, The Heritage Foundation, February 10, 2014. Reprinted by permission.

As you read, consider the following questions:

1. How do mandatory minimum sentences eliminate the dishonesty that characterized sentencing for the majority of the twentieth century?
2. What two widely acknowledged problems with the criminal justice system do mandatory minimum sentences address?
3. What is the principal objection to mandatory minimum sentences?

O n the other hand, a number of parties defend the use of mandatory minimum terms of imprisonment. They argue that mandatory minimum sentences reflect a societal judgment that certain offenses demand a specified minimum sanction and thereby ensure that anyone who commits such a crime cannot avoid a just punishment.

A nation of more than 300 million people will necessarily have a tremendous diversity of views as to the heinousness of the conduct proscribed by today's penal codes, and a bench with hundreds of federal district court judges will reflect that diversity. The decision as to what penalty should be imposed on a category of offenders requires consideration of the range of penological justifications for punishment, such as retribution, deterrence, incapacitation, education, and rehabilitation. Legislatures are better positioned than judges to make those types of judgments,[43] and Americans trust legislatures with the authority to make the moral and empirical decisions about how severely forbidden conduct should be sanctioned. Accordingly, having Congress specify the minimum penalty for a specific crime or category of offenses is entirely consistent with the proper functioning of the legislature in the criminal justice processes.

Mandatory minimum sentences eliminate the dishonesty that characterized sentencing for the majority of the 20th century. For most of that period, Congress vested district courts with complete discretion to select the appropriate period of confinement for an offender while also granting parole officials the authority to decide precisely whether and when to release an inmate before the completion of his sentence.

That division of authority created the inaccurate impression that the public action of the judge at sentencing fixed the offender's punishment while actually leaving that decision to the judgment of parole officials who act outside of the view of the public. At the same time, Congress could escape responsibility for making the moral judgments necessary to decide exactly how much punishment should be inflicted upon an individual by passing that responsibility off to parties who are not politically accountable for their actions. The entire process reflected dishonesty and generated cynicism, which corrodes the professional and public respect necessary for the criminal justice system to be deemed a morally defensible exercise of governmental power.

Mandatory minimum sentences also address two widely acknowledged problems with the criminal justice system: sentencing disparity and unduly lenient sentences. Mandatory minimums guarantee that sentences are uniform throughout the federal system and ensure that individuals are punished commensurate with their moral culpability by hitching the sentence to the crime, not the person.[44]

In fact, the need to use mandatory minimums as a means of addressing sentencing variances has become more pressing in the wake of the Supreme Court's 2005 decision in *United States v. Booker*.[45] *Booker* excised provisions of the Sentencing Reform Act of 1984 that had made the Sentencing Guidelines binding upon federal judges.[46] The result, unfortunately, has been a return to the type of inconsistency that existed before that statute became law. According to the Department of Justice, *Booker* has precipitated a return to unbridled judicial discretion: "[For] offenses for which there are no mandatory minimums, sentencing decisions have become largely unconstrained."[47] *Booker* therefore threatens to resurrect the sentencing disparities that, 30 years ago, prompted Congress to

ONE STATE'S REPEAL

In New Hampshire, pretty much only rape and murder convictions can land a defendant behind bars for the rest of his or her life. Burglary? With a record? You might get fifteen years. Unless you're Kevin Balch.

As Balch's original trial attorney puts it, "This case absolutely stands out in my opinion as one of the most unfair and unjust sentences, ever."

Balch had a record of break-ins. After burglarizing a home in 2012 and taking six guns, a Grafton county prosecutor charged him as an armed career criminal, and she charged each gun as a separate offense. Because the legislature had passed a mandatory minimum of ten years for each offense, 33 year old Balch ended up getting 60 years in prison.

Now, New Hampshire lawmakers are considering repealing that mandatory minimum sentencing law, as well as two others. It's part of a national movement to repeal mandatory minimum sentences after federal-level research showed they don't improve public safety but do disproportionately incarcerate people of color.

Attorney Len Harden says, for Balch, the mandatory minimum laws meant the judge's hands were tied.

"A young man was sentenced to serve essentially a life sentence for committing burglaries without any violence to any person or injuring anybody."

The state Supreme Court upheld Balch's 60-year sentence. But in their decision, they wrote, "We invite the legislature to reexamine the severe penalties" that result from mandatory minimums.

That is what the legislature is doing.

Since the 1980's, lawmakers have put thirty mandatory minimum sentences on the books in New Hampshire. This bill would eliminate three. Minimums for armed career criminals like Balch, though cases like his are rare. Also up for debate are mandatory minimums for habitual driving offenders and people who are caught driving without a license—both far more common.

An earlier version the bill eliminated all mandatory minimums, including drug offenses and DUIs.

During a recent Senate Judiciary hearing, a committee member asked co-sponsor, Representative Renny Cushing: if mandatory minimums don't work, why not do away with them all?

"Some of the crimes we opted not to remove are frankly high-profile hot button issues. We decided not to take up sex offenders. Drug dealing."

This bill is backed by both Republicans and Democrats. It's endorsed by the ACLU, the state defense attorney's lobby, as well as by the majority of people on a statewide criminal and juvenile justice council.

"N.H. Lawmakers Consider Repealing Some Mandatory Minimum Sentences," by Emily Corwin, New Hampshire Public Radio, March 28, 2016.

enact the Sentencing Reform Act. Mandatory minimum sentences may be the only way to eliminate that disparity today.

Mandatory minimum sentences also prevent crime because certain and severe punishment inevitably will have a deterrent effect.[48] Locking up offenders also incapacitates them for the term of their imprisonment and thereby protects the public.[49] In fact, where the chance of detection is low, as it is in the case of most drug offenses, reliance on fixed, lengthy prison sentences is preferable to a discretionary sentencing structure because mandatory sentences enable communities to conserve scarce enforcement resources without losing any deterrent benefit.[50]

Finally, the available evidence supports those conclusions. The 1990s witnessed a significant drop in crime across all categories of offenses,[51] and the mandatory minimum sentences adopted in the 1980s contributed to that decline.[52]

Moreover, mandatory minimums are an important law enforcement tool. They supply the police and prosecutors with the leverage necessary to secure the cooperation and testimony of low-level offenders against their more senior confederates.[53] The evidence shows that mandatory minimums, together with the Sentencing Guidelines promulgated by the US Sentencing Commission, have produced more cooperation and accomplice testimony in organized crime cases.[54]

It is a mistake to condemn mandatory minimum sentences because of the cost of imprisoning offenders. Opponents of mandatory minimums decry the high cost of housing a large number of inmates for a lengthy period of time and point to other criminal justice programs—e.g., the FBI, Federal Public Defenders, and victim advocates—that can better use those funds. That argument, however, does not consider both sides of the ledger. Imprisonment reduces the number of future victims of crime and thereby reduces the costs that they and the rest of society would otherwise suffer. Society is entitled to decide how to spend its funds, and underwriting the cost of incapacitating proven criminals is certainly a legitimate use of resources. Moreover, this efficiency-based criticism mistakenly assumes that Congress will not increase the budget for the Justice Department to use a valuable criminal justice tool: imprisonment.

In any event, there is no guarantee that any funds saved by reducing the length of offenders' sentences will go to other components of the criminal justice system. Indeed, there is no criminal justice "lockbox" into which all saved or unspent funds are dumped, and it is dishonest to pretend that funds not given to the Federal Bureau of Prisons will necessarily be used elsewhere in the criminal justice system rather than for non–criminal justice government programs.

Finally, the arguments against mandatory minimum sentences are, at their core, just a sleight of hand. The principal objection to mandatory minimum sentences is not that they are mandatory, but that they are severe or that they are required for drug offenses. No one would object to a mandatory 30-day sentence for possession of heroin or a mandatory one-year sentence for rape (in fact, the objection likely would be that those mandatory sentences are too short). Critics are concerned less about the mandatory nature of federal sentences than they are about their length and their use in drug cases.

Endnotes

43. *See, e.g., Gregg v. Georgia*, 428 U.S. 153, 186 (1976) (lead opinion).

44. *See, e.g.*, Mandatory Minimum Penalties, *supra* note 21; Prepared Statement of David B. Muhlhausen, Senior Policy Analyst, Heritage Foundation, to the U.S. Sentencing Comm'n 9 (May 27, 2010).

45. 543 U.S. 220 (2005).

46. *See, e.g.*, Paul J. Larkin, Jr., Parole: Corpse or Phoenix?, 50 *Am. Crim. L. Rev.* 303, 321–26 (2013).

47. Prepared Statement of Sally Quillian Yates, U.S. Attorney, Northern District of Georgia, to the U.S. Sentencing Comm'n 7 (May 27, 2010).

48. *See, e.g.*, Steven N. Durlauf & Daniel S. Nagin, *Imprisonment and Crime: Can Both Be Reduced?*, 10 Criminology & Pub. Pol'y 13, 37–38 (2011); Charles R. Tittle & Alan R. Rowe, *Certainty of Arrest and Crime Rates: A Further Test of the Deterrence Hypothesis*, 52 Soc. Forces 455 (June 1974).

49. *See, e.g.*, Shlomo Shinnar & Reuel Shinnar, *The Effects of the Criminal Justice System on the Control of Crime: A Quantitative Approach*, 9 Law & Soc'y Rev. 581 (1975)); Robert S. Mueller III, *Mandatory Minimum Sentencing*, 4 Fed. Sent'g Rep. 230 (1992).

50. *See, e.g.*, Gary S. Becker, *Crime and Punishment: An Economic Approach*, 76 J. Pol. Econ. 169, 178–85 (1968); Richard A. Posner, *An Economic Theory of the Criminal Law*, 85 Colum. L. Rev. 1193, 1212–13 (1985).

51. *See* Steven D. Levitt, *Understanding Why Crime Fell in the 1990s*, 18 J. of Econ. Persp. 163, 163 (2004).

52. *See* Stanley Sporkin & Asa Hutchinson, Debate, *Mandatory Minimums in Drug Sentencing: A Valuable Weapon in the War on Drugs or a Handcuff on Judicial Discretion?*, 36 Am. Crim. L. Rev. 1279, 1283 (1999).

53. *See Reevaluating the Effectiveness of Federal Mandatory Minimum Sentences: Hearing Before the S. Comm. on the Judiciary*, 113th Cong. 3 (2013); Prepared Statement of Raymond W. Kelly, Commissioner, New York Police Department, to the U.S. Sentencing Comm'n 4 (July 10, 2009).

54. *See, e.g.*, John C. Jeffries, Jr., & John Gleeson, *The Federalization of Organized Crime: Advantages of Federal Prosecution*, 46 Hastings L.J. 1095, 1119–21 (1995).

> "A nonviolent marijuana grower with no ties to gangs or drug-trafficking organizations ... can receive a sentence exponentially longer than a man who caused irreversible trauma to an innocent young girl."

Mandatory Minimum Sentences Are Cruel and Ineffective

Taylor Auten

In the following viewpoint, Taylor Auten argues that our criminal justice system is "convoluted" when somebody merely growing an illegal plant can receive a harsher sentence than a person convicted of rape. The author offers an overview of drug-related mandatory minimum sentences in the United States and several examples of their harsh effects. Auten claims, "Mandatory minimum sentencing for nonviolent drug infractions turns the criminal justice system into a machine for chewing up and spitting out those who suffer from addiction, punishing them instead of rehabilitating them." She points out the strong public opposition with "77 percent of citizens stating they were against it in 2015." Taylor Auten is a US section staff writer and associate editor for the Brown Political Review.

"Minimum Sentence, Mandatory Damage," by Taylor Auten, Originally published in the *Brown Political Review*, October 24, 2016. Reprinted by permission.

As you read, consider the following questions:

1. When did the modern story of drug-related mandatory minimum sentencing in the United States begin?
2. What are some examples of the harsh effects of mandatory minimum sentencing laws?
3. How strong is public opposition to mandatory minimum sentencing?

O n September 11, 2015, 75-year-old Lee Carroll Brooker, a disabled war veteran with chronic pain, received the news he had been dreading for months; his Supreme Court petition, challenging his life sentence for growing three dozen marijuana plants, had been denied. "[If the court] could sentence you to a term that is less than life without parole, I would," said trial Judge Larry Anderson of the draconian sentence. But, as Judge Anderson's comments indicate, he could not. His hands were tied by an Alabama state law that imposed a mandatory minimum sentence of life in prison for anyone caught with more than 2.2 pounds of marijuana who had been previously convicted of a felony. That was the case for Brooker, who had been convicted of a felony more than three decades prior. In contrast to Brooker's sentence, on October 12, 2016, Martin Joseph Blake was sentenced to 60 days in jail for repeatedly raping his 12-year-old daughter.

This shocking comparison offers an illuminating insight into the convoluted nature of the United States criminal justice system: a nonviolent marijuana grower with no ties to gangs or drug-trafficking organizations, merely growing the plant for his own personal use, can receive a sentence exponentially longer than a man who caused irreversible trauma to an innocent young girl. The issue at hand is mandatory minimum sentencing laws, standards set by legislative bodies that require a minimum number of years in prison for people convicted of certain crimes. In the US, the most controversial examples of these laws apply to drugs. Mandatory minimums effectively strip the judge of any discretion he or she might have to impose a sentence that is proportionate to the crime committed, and that is "sufficient, but not greater than necessary" to reflect the seriousness of the offense, promote respect for the law, and provide just punishment for the offense.

The modern story of drug-related mandatory minimum sentencing in the United States began with the passage of the Anti-Drug Abuse Act of 1986. In the wake of the cocaine overdose death of Len Bias, the second overall pick in the 1986 NBA draft, Congress swiftly passed the act, bypassing the usual deliberative steps of committee hearings. Although the "War on Drugs" began rhetorically with President Nixon in 1971, the Anti-Drug Abuse Act of 1986 marked the first major legislative effort since his declaration to give teeth to this claim. The basic premise of the Act was to make the punishment for drug-related crimes harsher, which, in turn, would deter the proliferation of drug abuse throughout the Country. The legislature did this by introducing mandatory minimum sentences. In so doing, Congress changed the nature of drug related criminal justice from rehabilitative to punitive.

Over the years, Congress has passed a variety of legislative initiatives modifying these mandatory minimums, changing the number of years required for certain quantities and particular drugs. One of the most punitive of these laws was Section 851 of United States Code 21, which allows for a person charged in federal court to face an enhanced mandatory minimum sentence if he or she has a prior felony conviction, and the prosecutor chooses to file what is known as a "prior felony information" or "PFI." This is an extremely powerful tool for prosecutors. A first-time marijuana grower facing 5 or 10 years might decide to try his luck at trial. But that same man with a prior felony, facing the threat of 20 years or life, might have a different viewpoint. The use of PFIs became so prolific that in 2013, then-Attorney General Eric Holder released a memo instructing federal prosecutors to use PFIs only in the most severe cases, where the defendant has exhibited violent behavior, is among the leadership of a gang or drug trafficking organization, or has a significant criminal history.

Examples of the harsh effects of mandatory minimum sentencing laws are not hard to find. On May 9, 1999, Tyrone Taylor sold $20 of crack cocaine to an undercover officer. Unfortunately, Taylor had been caught selling the drug twice earlier in his life, and was required to serve a life in prison. Joseph Tigano III, a non-violent man living peacefully in rural Western New York, was caught operating a marijuana grow house, for which he received a mandatory minimum 20-year sentence based on a prior conviction, more than a decade earlier, for growing 10 marijuana plants. Indeed, the judge described the sentence as "much greater than is necessary" and lamented that she had "no choice."

Mandatory minimum sentencing for non-violent drug infractions turns the criminal justice system into a machine for chewing up and spitting out those who suffer from addiction, punishing them instead of rehabilitating them. Rather than treating those affected by their toxic grasp as enemy combatants to be thrown in prison in a "war on drugs," drug addiction should be treated as a public health problem, and treatment given to those affected by it. Legal scholar Mark Osler frames the situation well: "If we take a rapist away from society and stop him from raping women, that is a good thing. If we take a very low-level crack dealer out of the society and imprison him for life, that's not solving any problem because it's a market. And you don't solve a market problem by sweeping up low-wage labor."

Fortunately, unlike many controversial and partisan issues that tend to split Congress and the nation, public opposition to mandatory minimum sentencing is strong, with 77 percent of citizens stating they were against it in 2015. It is also generally agreed upon as an ineffective deterrent to crime. A report from the Federal Judicial Center stated, "Trends in criminal victimization rates and drug availability for the periods before and after the mandatory minimums took effect fail to demonstrate any reduction in crime that can be attributed to the mandatory minimums."

Regrettably, Congress has been incapable of passing the necessary criminal justice reform to put an end to this issue. The

Sentencing Reform and Corrections Act of 2015, a bill presented to Congress in the fall of 2015, would have been a step in the right direction, reducing many of the mandatory minimums for many drug related crimes. Unfortunately, the Republican party has been heavily split on the issue. Spearheading the movement against the bipartisan push for criminal justice reform is Senator Tom Cotton (R-AR), a graduate of both Harvard College and Harvard Law School, who argues that, despite the United States having the largest prison population in the world, "we have an under-incarceration problem." He rejects the notions that those convicted of crimes should be given sympathy, also stating "As for the claim that we should have more empathy for criminals, I won't even try to conceal my contempt for the idea." Sadly, to date, the bill has yet to pass. Cotton's efforts, collaborating with others, have succeeded enough to cause majority leader Mitch McConnell (R-KY) to not yet make a commitment to bring the issue onto the table, and key authors of the bill like Senator Richard Durbin (D-IL) have declared it to be "over."

Given this legislative inaction, it's important to consider the role and powers of the executive. Former Attorney General Holder took the right step by asking prosecutors to pursue mandatory minimums enhancements only in the most severe cases. In addition, the President has the power to commute or pardon federal prisoners. President Obama has already begun to take the necessary steps towards reversing the injustice caused by mandatory minimum sentences by making use of his clemency power more than any other President before him. Thus far, he has commuted the sentences of 673 inmates—325 in this August alone. But that is not enough. Directives need to be given to law enforcement to shift focus away from petty drug crimes. The United States boasts an exorbitant 192,170 inmates in its federal prison system alone, with 46.4 percent jailed for drug offenses. While certainly not all of these inmates deserve exoneration, many of them are unjustly serving sentences that they would not even receive if they were sentenced today.

With the 2016 election looming in the foreground, the future of clemency initiatives is uncertain. President Obama has taken good first steps, but momentum for progress could be lost if the next administration scales back clemency efforts. Secretary Clinton has come out in favor of reforming mandatory minimum sentencing laws, which would both continue to give presidential support for Congressional action and would indicate that she would be amenable to continuing President Obama's actions on clemency. Donald Trump has emphasized law and order, and has expressed support for mandatory minimum sentencing laws for immigrants convicted of illegal entry. These combine to suggest that Trump is unlikely to partner with those who seek to reduce or eliminate mandatory minimums for drug crimes.

Above all, one thing is clear: until the legislature can unite to address this issue, the executive remains the most effectual branch in producing change on mandatory minimums. Across the country, judges' hands are tied as they are forced to hand severe sentences that bear no relation to the crime committed. With only a few weeks until the 2016 election, voters should keep criminal justice policy central in their minds as they consider for whom to vote up and down the ballot. As this administration has shown, executive action can have some positive impact, but it cannot provide a structural fix to this problem. This election has so far only stalled progress on what was once a promising effort to address this irrevocable injustice; it would be a welcome turn of events for the results of this election to harken a new era of bipartisan criminal justice reform that restores justice into our perhaps inaptly-named "justice system."

> *"Studies have found time and time
> again that harsher punishments
> and the higher incarceration rates
> they lead to don't have a big impact
> on crime."*

There Is No Evidence to Support Harsh Punishments for Drug Offenses

German Lopez

In the following viewpoint, German Lopez argues that studies have found harsh punishments, such as mandatory minimum sentences, and higher incarceration rates do not have a big impact on crime, and that: "longer stints in prison can actually lead to more crime." He states that "harsh mandatory minimums for drug offenses don't even seem to have an impact on the flow of drugs." Studies indicate that there is no evidence that harsher punishments do a better job than lighter penalties. The author contends that the federal government doesn't have a big impact on crime because most policy is done at the state and local levels. German Lopez has written for Vox since its launch in 2014, with a focus on drugs, guns, criminal justice, race, and LGBTQ issues.

"Jeff Sessions: Mandatory Minimum Sentences Protected Us from Violent Crime. Research: Nope, by German Lopez, Vox Media, July 11, 2017. https://www.vox.com/policy-and-politics/2017/7/11/15955570/jeff-sessionsmandatory-minimums-crime. Reprinted by permission.

As you read, consider the following questions:

1. Do harsh mandatory minimums for drug offenses seem to have an impact on the flow of drugs?
2. What is the fundamental problem with the argument Attorney General Sessions is making, according to the viewpoint author?
3. What caused the rise in violent crime over the past two years?

Attorney General Jeff Sessions's latest explanation for the rise in violent crime is, well, exactly what you would expect from the head of President Donald Trump's "tough on crime" agenda.

In comments at a conference for the anti-drug program DARE, Sessions referenced a memo by the Obama administration that told federal prosecutors to avoid charges for low-level drug offenders that could trigger lengthy mandatory minimums. He argued that this memo caused violent crime to spike for the first time in decades—and suggested his decision to revoke the memo will, in turn, cause violent crime to fall:

> Under the previous administration, the Department of Justice told federal prosecutors not to include in charging documents the full amount of drugs being dealt when the actual amount would trigger a mandatory minimum sentence. Prosecutors were required to leave out true facts in order to achieve sentences lighter than required by law. This was billed as an effort to curb "mass incarceration" of "low-level offenders," but in reality it covered offenders apprehended with large quantities of dangerous drugs.
>
> What was the result? It was exactly what you would think: sentences went down and crime went up. Sentences for federal drug crimes dropped by 18 percent from 2009 to 2016. Violent crime—which had been decreasing for two decades—suddenly went up again. Two years after this policy change, the United States suffered the largest single-year increase in the overall violent crime rate since 1991.

These claims ignore years and years of empirical research on this exact question—including some research done by US Department of Justice, which Sessions now heads.

In short, studies have found time and time again that harsher punishments—which mandatory minimums force on judges by requiring that they sentence offenders to a minimum amount of time in prison—and the higher incarceration rates they lead to don't have a big impact on crime.

A 2015 review of the research by the Brennan Center for Justice estimated that more incarceration explained 0 to 7 percent of the crime drop since the 1990s, while other researchers estimate it drove 10 to 25 percent of the crime drop since the '90s—not a big impact either way. A 2014 analysis by the Pew Charitable Trusts also found that states that reduced their imprisonment rates also saw some of the biggest drops in crime, suggesting that there isn't a hard link between incarceration and crime.

In fact, longer stints in prison can actually lead to more crime. As the National Institute of Justice—an agency within the Justice Department—concluded in 2016, "Research shows clearly that the chance of being caught is a vastly more effective deterrent than even draconian punishment. … Research has found evidence that prison can exacerbate, not reduce, recidivism. Prisons themselves may be schools for learning to commit crimes."

Harsh mandatory minimums for drug offenses don't even seem to have an impact on the flow of drugs. A 2014 study from Peter Reuter at the University of Maryland and Harold Pollack at the University of Chicago found there's no good evidence that tougher punishments or harsher supply-elimination efforts do a better job of driving down access to drugs and substance abuse than lighter penalties. So increasing the severity of the punishment doesn't do much, if anything, to slow the flow of drugs.

More broadly, there's a fundamental problem with the argument Sessions is making: The federal government just doesn't have that much impact on crime. Most criminal justice policy is done at the state and local levels, where roughly 87 percent of prison inmates reside. As John Roman, a criminal justice expert at the University of Chicago, told me, "Federal drug sentencing affects the custody of only a tiny proportion of US offenders, so inferring a large, national increase in violence to any change in federal sentencing policy focuses on a butterfly effect rather than a direct cause."

This isn't the first time Sessions has made a comment like this. Previously, he said that New York City is "soft on crime" and as a result "continues to see gang murder after gang murder," because it has adopted various criminal justice reforms. In reality, New York has seen its crime rate fall in the past few years—and its homicide rate is now below the national average.

So far, the Justice Department has not provided evidence to support Sessions's claims.

So what did cause the rises in violent crime over the past two years? The short answer is criminologists don't really know yet. The most prominent, but unproven, explanation so far is that rising distrust in police, as well as police pulling back from proactive work in fear of mounting criticisms, led to more crime.

But it's also possible, criminologists say, that the violent crime rise could be temporary statistical fluctuations—as occurred in 2005 and 2006—or caused by something we just don't know about yet.

> *"Lots of crimes can be punished with alternative sentences that don't include jail or prison time."*

Alternative Sentences Are the Answer

FindLaw

In the following viewpoint, the authors at FindLaw examine the varied alternatives of criminal conviction. Many have argued that alternative sentences would be more effective in many cases than mandatory minimum sentences. The authors illustrate several different outcomes from the traditional prison sentence upon conviction of a crime. Alternative sentences can include different combinations of the following: a suspended sentence, probation, fines, restitution, community service, and deferred adjudication/ pretrial diversion. Any number of these can help relieve the problem of prison overcrowding. FindLaw is a division of Thomson Reuters that offers online law services and information for individuals and legal professionals.

As you read, consider the following questions:

1. What are some of the forms alternative sentences can take?
2. How is restitution like a fine?
3. Is it possible to have charges dismissed if the defendant completes specified conditions?

"Alternative Sentences," Thomson Reuters. Reprinted by permission.

S entences for a criminal conviction can take many forms, and a conviction doesn't always mean a trip to jail or prison. Alternative sentences can include different combinations of the following: a suspended sentence, probation, fines, restitution, community service and deferred adjudication/pretrial diversion. Judges typically determine whether to impose alternative sentences based on the type and severity of the crime, the age of the defendant, the defendant's criminal history, the effect of the crime on the victims, and the defendant's remorse. The articles below explore the different types of alternative sentences in more detail.

Suspended Sentences

As an alternative to imprisonment, a judge can issue a suspended sentence where he or she either refrains from handing down a sentence or decides on a sentence but refrains from carrying it out. This is generally reserved for less serious crimes or first-time offenders. Suspended sentences can be unconditional or conditional. An unconditional suspended sentence simply suspends the sentence with no strings attached.

If the suspended sentence is conditional, the judge can hold off from either imposing or executing the punishment so long as the defendant fulfills the condition of the suspension. Common conditions can include enrolling in a substance abuse program and not committing any further crimes. If the conditions aren't met, the judge can then either impose or execute a sentence.

Probation

Another alternative to prison is probation. Similar to a suspended sentence, probation releases a defendant back into the community, but he or she does not have the same level of freedom as a normal citizen. Courts typically grant probation for first-time or low-risk offenders. Statutes determine when probation is possible, but it is up to the sentencing judge to determine whether or not to actually grant probation.

Probation comes with conditions that restrict behavior, and if the probationer violates one of those conditions, the court may revoke or modify the probation. Courts have a great deal of discretion when imposing probation conditions.

Fines

Almost all of us have had to pay a fine once or twice, most often in the form of a speeding or parking ticket. People convicted of more serious crimes also have to pay fines in many situations, although the amount of the fine is usually much more substantial than a traffic ticket. Generally, fines are imposed to punish the offender, help compensate the state for the offense, and deter any future criminal acts.

Restitution

Restitution is like a fine, but the payment made by the perpetrator of a crime goes to the victims of that crime instead of the court or municipality. Judges often order restitution be paid in cases where victims suffered some kind of financial setback as the result of a crime. The payment is designed to make the victims whole and restore them financially to the point they were at prior to the commission of the crime.

For example, a graffiti artist who spray paints the side of a business may be ordered to pay restitution to the business owners who could then repaint the building. In another example, a defendant who injured his victim in a fight may be ordered to compensate the victim for his medical expenses.

Court Ordered Community Service

In some cases, a judge will order a criminal offender to perform work on behalf of the community, usually in exchange for a reduction of fines and/or incarceration. Court ordered community service can accompany some other form of alternative sentence with the intent that performing community service offers more

Repeal Mandatory Minimums

The United States Congress should adopt a blue ribbon task force's recommendation to repeal most federal mandatory minimum sentences for drug offenses, Human Rights Watch said today. The Charles Colson Task Force, a congressionally created body with the mandate to examine overcrowding in the federal prison system, presented its findings to Congress on February 1, 2016.

In a 132-page report, the task force unanimously urged Congress to reserve federal prisons for the most serious offenders, finding that federal sentences are "often substantially greater than necessary" and that mandatory minimum sentencing laws were a primary driver of that imbalance. To that end, it recommended eliminating a vast majority of mandatory minimum sentences for drug offenses—making an exception only for drug "kingpins" participating in continuing criminal enterprises.

"Congress asked the experts, and the experts agree that drug mandatory minimums belong on the chopping block," said Antonio Ginatta, US advocacy director at Human Rights Watch. "Federal mandatory minimums result in grossly disproportionate sentences, and there's no way to address prison overcrowding without tackling them."

The task force recommended applying the repeal of federal mandatory minimums retroactively, and that if Congress decides to enact future mandatory minimums of any kind, the requirement should automatically expire after five years.

Human Rights Watch recommended the elimination of all drug-related mandatory minimums 16 years ago in its report, "Punishment and Prejudice: Racial Disparities in the War on Drugs." Judges should be able to exercise their informed judgment in crafting proportionate and effective sentences for drug offenders. Mandatory minimums make this impossible. They force judges to sentence offenders without adequate regard to the particular circumstances of their case, often resulting in disproportionate sentences for relatively minor crimes. Enforcement of US drug laws disproportionately affects racial minorities, and mandatory minimums greatly compound the impact of that broader disparity.

The task force, named for Charles Colson, the founder of the largest prison ministry in the US, also made other significant

> recommendations. It recommended that any person who has served 15 years in prison should have the ability to apply for resentencing before a judicial authority. It also recommended that the Bureau of Prisons should do more to promote family engagement, by housing inmates close to home and facilitating family visits, to improve reentry into the community and reduce recidivism.
>
> Human Rights Watch, alongside 36 other organizations, supported the creation of the task force in 2013.
>
> **"US: Repeal Mandatory Federal Drug Sentences Task Force Recommends Sweeping Prison Reform," Human Rights Watch, February 2, 2016.**

benefit to society than being incarcerated. The community benefits from the work that the offender performs and avoids the cost of incarceration while the offender benefits from a lesser sentence and hopefully learns from his or her work experience.

Deferred Adjudication / Pretrial Diversion

Certain types of offenses and offenders may qualify for programs that result in having charges dismissed if the defendant completes specified conditions. Sometimes called deferred adjudication or diversion, these programs take the defendant out of the ordinary process of prosecution so he or she can complete certain conditions. Once he or she is done, either the prosecutor or the court dismisses the charges.

The goal of diversion programs is to allow a defendant time to demonstrate that they are capable of behaving responsibly, and they are typically used for drug offenses or first-time offenders. Normally, the conditions imposed include some form of counseling and/or probation, and require the defendant to stay out of trouble.

More Information

Every criminal case is different, and it is often difficult to know whether you're eligible for an alternative sentence or which ones a court may impose. If you've been charged with a crime, you may want to consult with an experienced criminal attorney in your area. You can also visit FindLaw's criminal law section for more general information on this topic.

Have a Criminal Defense Attorney Review Your Case for Free

Lots of crimes can be punished with alternative sentences that don't include jail or prison time. No matter what criminal matter you're considering or facing, only an expert criminal defense attorney can be relied on to explain your state's laws to help you predict your best course of action. If you're being investigated or charged with a crime, you should immediately contact a criminal defense attorney for a free case review to better understand your situation.

Periodical and Internet Sources Bibliography

The following articles have been selected to supplement the diverse views presented in this chapter.

Denise M. Champagne, "N.Y. Senate Hears Call for Federal Sentencing Reform," *Daily Record* (Rochester, NY). September 20, 2013.

"EDITORIAL: Mandatory Minimum Sentencing Under Fire," *Frederick News-Post,* January 9, 2014. https://www .fredericknewspost.com/news/crime_and_justice/courts/ mandatory-minimum-sentencing-under-fire/article_4915b032-a7bc-545a-b800-b50d100f5691.html.

"EDITORIAL: "Pass Crucial Justice Reform," *Times-Tribune,* December 9, 2017. http://thetimes-tribune.com/opinion/pass-crucial-justice-reform-1.2277056.

"EDITORIAL: Sentencing Reform Pays Dividends," *Mail Tribune* (Medford, OR), December 11, 2014. http://www.mailtribune .com/article/20141211/opinion/141219931.

Tom Egan, "Criminal - Crack - Sentencing," *Rhode Island Lawyers Weekly*, May 12, 2015.

Zeninjor Enwemeka, "4 Things to Know About the Mass. Debate on Mandatory Minimum Sentences," by WBUR.org, June 10, 2015. http://www.wbur.org/news/2015/06/10/mandatory-minimum-sentences-primer.

Donald J. Lampard and Christine Smith, "Oklahoma Passes Four Criminal Justice Reform Measures," American Legislative Exchange Council, May 2, 2016. https://www.alec.org/article/ oklahoma-passes-four-criminal-justice-reform-measures.

Pew Charitable Trusts, Fact Sheet: Growth in Federal Prison System Exceeds States', January 22, 2015, http://www.pewtrusts.org/en/ research-and-analysis/fact-sheets/2015/01/growth-in-federal-prison-system-exceeds-states.

Craig Turner, "Kant's Categorical Imperative and Mandatory Minimum Sentencing," *Washington University Jurisprudence Review*, Volume 8, Issue 2, 2016. http://openscholarship. wustl.edu/cgi/viewcontent.cgi?article=1143&context=law_ jurisprudence.

OPPOSING
VIEWPOINTS®
SERIES

CHAPTER 2

Who Should Decide How Long a Mandatory Sentence Should Be?

Chapter Preface

P unishments are intended to be proportional to the crime. Sentencing guidelines suggest a range of sentences appropriate for various types of crimes. Judges need not adhere strictly, but can consider any mitigating or aggravating circumstances related to the specific crime, such as whether the perpetrator was the principal offender or just an accessory, whether anybody was hurt or the perpetrator actively tried to avoid hurting anybody, or the perpetrator's mental state at the time of the crime. The final sentence may be within the suggested range but could also be shorter or longer at the judge's discretion. With mandatory minimum sentences, a judge is not permitted to impose a shorter sentence even if there are facts that would normally provide a reason for leniency.

Federal mandatory minimum sentencing statutes demand incarceration or execution after a criminal conviction, but they circumscribe judicial sentencing discretion while they impose few limits upon a prosecutor's discretion, or the president's power to pardon. They have been criticized as too harsh and incompatible with a rational sentencing guideline system, yet still embraced as bastions of truth in sentencing and a certain way to incapacitate the dangerous criminals.

Mandatory minimum sentences have not eliminated sentencing disparities because they have not eliminated sentencing discretion: They have merely shifted that discretion from judges to prosecutors. Judges have to impose whatever punishment the law requires, but prosecutors are under no comparable obligation to charge a defendant with violating a law carrying a mandatory minimum penalty.

Former Detroit mayor and Michigan Supreme Court Justice Dennis W. Archer takes the position that "it is time for America to stop getting tougher and start getting smarter against crime by reassessing mandatory minimum sentencing and irrevocable prison terms." In an article posted on the American Bar Association's website, he states, "The idea that Congress can dictate a one-size-fits-all sentencing scheme does not make sense. Judges need to have the discretion to weigh the specifics of the cases before them and determine an appropriate sentence. There is a reason we give judges a gavel, not a rubber stamp." Also, Congress must ask itself: With respect to each crime, is justice best served by having legislatures assign fixed penalties to that crime? Or should legislatures leave judges more or less free to tailor sentences to the aggravating and mitigating facts of each criminal case within a defined range?

> "Most people would agree that
> the government should be free to
> incentivize clearly guilty defendants
> to forego trials. Yet a 75 percent
> discount (or penalty, depending on
> your perspective) seems completely
> out of whack."

The Judicial Branch Should Decide What a Mandatory Minimum Sentence Should Be

Kevin Ring

In the following viewpoint, Kevin Ring questions mandatory minimum sentences set by Congress, stating: "The problem is that federal mandatory minimum sentencing penalties cannot possibly be expected to fit the facts and circumstances of every case in perpetuity." While supporters of mandatory minimums likely would argue that these laws worked exactly how they are supposed to, most people would agree that the government should be free to incentivize clearly guilty defendants to forego trials. He feels that: "Congress should eliminate mandatory minimums so that all Americans can be punished the same way." Kevin Ring is vice president of Families Against Mandatory Minimums (FAMM).

"Congress should learn from staffer's sentencing," by Kevin Ring, First appeared in the hill, Capitol Hill Publishing Corporation, January 27, 2016. Reprinted by permission.

As you read, consider the following questions:

1. Why was Senate Appropriations Committee staffer Fred Pagan sentenced to prison?
2. What is the problem with federal mandatory minimum sentencing penalties, as stated in the viewpoint?
3. How should the US justice system work, according to the viewpoint author?

E arlier this month, former Senate Appropriations Committee staffer Fred Pagan was sentenced to prison for buying a steady supply of methamphetamine over the course of many years. Pagan's crime was serious and clearly the product of addiction. Beside Pagan's guilt, the one thing everyone in the courtroom at his sentencing appeared to agree on was that ten years in federal prison—the mandatory minimum prison term established by Congress—would have been far too severe a punishment for his crime.

Pagan's lawyers argued that his drug addiction and abusive childhood mitigated his culpability. Pointing also to Pagan's 30 years of exemplary service as a Hill staffer, the lawyers said that a sentence of probation (along with the high profile shaming he had already endured) would be adequate punishment. Judge Beryl Howell, another former Senate staffer, ultimately sentenced Pagan to two-and-a-half years in prison. The prosecution seemed content with the outcome. Justice was served.

But, wait. Let's take a step back. If Pagan's sentencing was right—and I've heard no one complain it was too lenient—what does that say about the mandatory minimum sentence set by Congress? After all, Pagan's sentence of two-and-a-half years was 75 percent lower than the ten-year statutory minimum that applied to his crime.

Supporters of mandatory minimums likely would argue that these laws worked exactly how they are supposed to. Threatened with the prospect of spending a full decade in prison, Pagan quickly accepted responsibility for his crime, thereby saving the government from having to conduct a trial, and cooperated with law enforcement. Pagan's decision certainly saved taxpayers from paying for an unnecessary trial and might lead to the apprehension of others in the drug business.

These public benefits, however, say nothing at all about Pagan's culpability or moral blameworthiness, which are the proper bases of his punishment. Had Pagan chosen for whatever reason to exercise his constitutional right to make the government prove his guilt beyond a reasonable doubt to a jury of his peers, a sentence of ten years would not have suddenly become reasonable. Not even the prosecutors thought society would be safer with the longer sentence—but they would have pursued it but for the fact that Pagan gave up his rights.

Most people would agree that the government should be free to incentivize clearly guilty defendants to forego trials. Yet a 75 percent discount (or penalty, depending on your perspective) seems completely out of whack.

The problem is that federal mandatory minimum sentencing penalties cannot possibly be expected to fit the facts and circumstances of every case in perpetuity. Members of Congress are not clairvoyant. Moreover, mandatory minimums do not even pretend to reflect an offender's culpability or role in the offense. They are driven by one factor, and in the case of drugs that factor is quantity. And since people are usually charged as members of a conspiracy, they typically are held responsible not just for the quantity of drugs they personally used, sold, or possessed, but also for the quantity of everyone else in the alleged conspiracy. This practice exposes a bit player to the same mandatory sentence as a kingpin. Even worse, the kingpin often can escape the mandatory minimum sentence because he is more likely to have more useful information to share with prosecutors—and can therefore secure a better deal at sentencing.

The absurd but predictable result? The US Sentencing Commission has found that street-level dealers and mules get sentenced to mandatory minimums more often than kingpins.

The Pagan case demonstrates how justice can be served better without federal mandatory minimums. Because prosecutors did not allege or prove a specific drug quantity in Pagan's case, he was spared from what everyone, including the prosecutors, agreed would have been an absurdly long sentence. The judge, informed by both sides of all the relevant factors in the case, and aware of what punishments similar offenders in similar cases have received, imposed a sentence that was within the federal sentencing guidelines.

Had Judge Howell ignored the guidelines completely and given Pagan a probation-only sentence without providing a reasonable justification for such leniency, prosecutors would have been free to appeal her decision. They likely would have prevailed, too, since the Justice Department wins its sentencing appeals 65 percent of the time, a fact rarely mentioned in sentencing reform debates.

This is how America's justice system should work. A society like ours that believes so deeply in personal responsibility should punish individuals as individuals. Pagan broke the law and deserved to be held accountable for his crime. As he alone was responsible for the actions that led to his prison sentence, it was only right that all of the relevant facts and circumstances of his crime and life were used to inform the sentence he was given. Congress should eliminate mandatory minimums so that all Americans can be punished the same way.

> *"Critics say these minimums disproportionately affect minorities and are part of the failed war on drugs, but Attorney General Jeff Sessions is instructing federal prosecutors to apply those minimums across the board, especially in drug cases."*

Judges Should Decide What Punishment Fits the Crime

Rachel Martin

In the following viewpoint, an interview with federal judge Mark Bennett, Rachel Martin questions the effect of mandatory minimum sentences, noting that they disproportionately affect minorities and are part of the failed War on Drugs. Judge Bennett says: "These mandatory minimums are so incredibly harsh, and they're triggered by such low levels of drugs that they snare at these non-violent, low-level addicts who are involved in drug distribution mostly to obtain drugs to feed their habit." He goes on to state: "I obviously have a very strong opposition to mandatory minimums. But when I was sworn in as a United States district court judge, I took an oath to uphold the law whether I agree with it or not." Rachel Martin is host of NPR's Morning Edition, as well as NPR's morning news podcast Up First.

As you read, consider the following questions:

1. What did Judge Bennett note about Attorney General Session's memo?
2. Does Judge Bennett think it really makes sense to treat a for-profit seller and a non-for-profit user the same?
3. What percentage of mandatory minimum sentences, in Judge Bennett's opinion, are unfair?

N PR's Rachel Martin speaks to federal Judge Mark Bennett of Iowa, who opposes mandatory minimum charging and sentencing guidelines for nonviolent drug offenses.

RACHEL MARTIN, HOST: We're continuing our conversation about criminal justice reform this week, specifically the effect of mandatory minimum sentencing. Critics say these minimums disproportionately affect minorities and are part of the failed war on drugs, but Attorney General Jeff Sessions is instructing federal prosecutors to apply those minimums across the board, especially in drug cases. Yesterday, we heard from Georgetown law professor and former prosecutor Bill Otis. He supports the Justice Department's policy.

BILL OTIS: The system of guidelines and mandatory minimums has been a big success if one judges the success of the criminal justice system by the crime rate rather than the incarceration rate.

MARTIN: Although some judges think the incarceration rate is a big part of the problem. Mark Bennett is one of them. He's a federal judge from Iowa's Northern District. Bennett says mandatory minimum laws have forced him to put more than a thousand people in prison for lengthy stays, sometimes for the rest of their lives. And in a majority of those cases, Judge Bennett says the punishment didn't fit the crime.

MARK BENNETT: These mandatory minimums are so incredibly harsh, and they're triggered by such low levels of drugs that they snare at these non-violent, low-level addicts who are involved in drug distribution mostly to obtain drugs to feed their habit. They have a medical problem. It's called addiction, and they're going to be faced with five and 10 and 20-year and sometimes life mandatory minimum sentences. I think that's a travesty.

MARTIN: So people who support this policy change will argue, as has Attorney General Sessions, that there's no real thing as a low-level drug crime, that inherently violence is kind of baked into this experience. If you want to collect a drug debt, Sessions says, you can't file a lawsuit in court. You collect it with the barrel of a gun. So how do you respond to that?

BENNETT: There's actually a very easy, simple response to that. Any one of my 660 federal district court judge colleagues when there's actual violence involved in a case will impose a higher sentence than if there was no violence involved in the case. So that's really a red herring argument. And, you know, when I read the—Attorney General Session's memo, I noticed he was talking about consistency and fairness.

MARTIN: Yeah. They argued that mandatory minimums help ensure consistency, and as a result, the laws become more egalitarian.

BENNETT: Yeah. Well, I think just the opposite is true. Mandatory minimums support unwarranted uniformity by treating everyone alike even though their situations are dramatically different. So, for example, you have a low-level non-violent drug offender. One is selling methamphetamine for profit, and one is using methamphetamine and maybe trading it to other drug addicts to support their addiction.

Does it really make sense to treat a for-profit seller and a non-for-profit user the same? I don't think so because Congress has also

The Safety Valve

Is justice best served by having legislatures assign fixed penalties to each crime? Or should legislatures leave judges more or less free to tailor sentences to the aggravating and mitigating facts of each criminal case within a defined range?

The proliferation in recent decades of mandatory minimum penalties for federal crimes, along with the tremendous increase in the prison population, has forced those concerned with criminal justice in America to reconsider this age-old question. The Supreme Court of the United States has upheld lengthy mandatory terms of imprisonment over the challenge that they violate the Eighth Amendment's prohibition against cruel and unusual punishments. The question remains, however, whether mandatory minimums are sound criminal justice policy.

Today [2014], public officials on both sides of the aisle support amending the federal mandatory minimum sentencing laws. Two bills with bipartisan support are currently under consideration. Senators Patrick Leahy (D–VT) and Rand Paul (R–KY) have introduced the Justice Safety Valve Act of 2013, which would apply to all federal mandatory minimums. Senators Dick Durbin (D–IL) and Mike Lee (R–UT) have introduced the Smarter Sentencing Act, which would apply to federal mandatory minimums for only drug offenses.

The bottom line is this: Each proposal might be a valuable step forward in criminal justice policy, but it is difficult to predict the precise impact that each one would have. This much, however, appears likely: The Smarter Sentencing Act is narrowly tailored to address one of the most pressing problems with mandatory minimums: severe sentences for relatively minor drug possession crimes. The so-called safety valve allows judges to avoid applying mandatory minimums, even absent substantial assistance. The safety valve, however, has a limited scope: It applies only to sentences imposed for nonviolent drug offenses where the offender meets specific criteria relating to criminal history, violence, lack of injury to others, and leadership.

"Reconsidering Mandatory Minimum Sentences: The Arguments for and Against Potential Reforms," by Paul Larkin and Evan Bernick, The Hertiage Foundation, 2014.

said we're supposed to look at the nature and circumstances of the offense and the history and characteristics of the defendant. And, in fact, I think it's important to go back and look at the history of the mandatory minimums.

They came about because Len Bias, a basketball player, died of powder cocaine overdose but everybody assumed it was crack. And that's what triggered this massive political ratcheting up and passing the mandatory minimums. And it wasn't just Democrats, and it wasn't just Republicans, they were outbidding each other trying to increase and ratchet up the mandatory minimums.

And the interesting thing is that bill passed without a single congressional hearing, not a single federal judge was called to testify, not a single person from the Federal Bureau of Prisons. There were no criminologists, no penologists, just no pharmacologists. And they picked these mandatory minimums and the drug quantities literally out of thin air.

MARTIN: Let me ask you, there have been some of your colleagues, some judges have felt so strongly about the mandatory minimums that they have resigned. They have stepped down from the bench in protest. Is that something you would consider doing? If not, why stay? Why do you find it to be more valuable to stay in your position?

BENNETT: Well, I've certainly thought about it because I obviously have a very strong opposition to mandatory minimums. But when I was sworn in as a United States district court judge, I took an oath to uphold the law whether I agree with it or not.

So the fact that I have a personal disagreement with not all mandatory minimums—some are justified—but in my judgment, about 80 percent of them are unfair, so I thought I could do more staying in the system. I respect the judges who have said they can no longer do it and decide to resign, but I'm not there yet.

MARTIN: Mark Bennett is a US district court judge for the Northern District of Iowa. Judge Bennett, thank you so much for talking with us.

BENNETT: Thank you so much, Rachel, for having me.

> *"Before 1984, federal sentencing was simultaneously simple and opaque. A judge could impose a sentence of any length—or none at all—'up to the maximums established in the statute defining the crime.'"*

Sentences Should Apply Equally Regardless of Who Committed the Crime

Jillian Hewitt

In the following excerpted viewpoint, Jillian Hewitt argues that between 1987 and 2005, federal judges sentenced defendants pursuant to binding sentencing guidelines that severely curtailed their discretion. In United States v. Booker, *the Supreme Court held the mandatory guidelines sentencing scheme unconstitutional and rendered the guidelines advisory. This article offers a picture of white-collar sentencing in "shades of gray." It conducts an empirical analysis of sentencing decisions after* Booker *to assess the consequences of the return to judicial discretion. In particular, the viewpoint examines major white-collar cases in the Southern District of New York, where many such cases of national and international significance are prosecuted. Jillian Hewitt is a graduate of Yale Law School. She has clerked in the US District Court for the Southern District of New York and is an associate at Susman Godfrey LLP.*

"Fifty Shades of Gray: Sentencing Trends in Major White-Collar Cases," by Jillian Hewitt, *The Yale Law Journal,* February 2016. Reprinted by permission.

As you read, consider the following questions:

1. How did the SRA radically alter the system by establishing binding guidelines that greatly reduced judicial discretion?
2. When did the first iteration of the sentencing guidelines promulgated by the Commission go into effect?
3. What does the existing literature acknowledge about the guidelines producing extraordinarily high sentences for white-collar offenders?

A. The Advent of the Sentencing Guidelines and the Mandatory Regime

Before 1984, federal sentencing was simultaneously simple and opaque. A judge could impose a sentence of any length—or none at all—"up to the maximums established in the statute defining the crime."[36] Judges were not required to consider any particular circumstances, nor were they required to explain their reasons for imposing a particular sentence.[37]

The SRA radically altered this system by establishing binding Guidelines that greatly reduced judicial discretion. In enacting the SRA, Congress sought to reduce "unwarranted" disparities in sentencing.[38] Congress passed the statute on the heels of a short yet influential book by Judge Marvin Frankel, *Criminal Sentences: Law Without Order*, published in 1973. Judge Frankel argued that unfettered judicial discretion in sentencing produced arbitrary outcomes whereby defendants who committed similar crimes received vastly different sentences. Frankel argued for the establishment of "an administrative sentencing commission 'of prestige and credibility,'"[39] which could create a "detailed chart or calculus" that would weigh the "many elements that go into the sentence"[40] and provide the judge with a narrow sentencing range from which the judge would choose a specific sentence.[41]

The SRA amended the federal sentencing process in several ways. Among other changes, it created the United States Sentencing

Commission, an independent agency in the judicial branch. The SRA instructed the Commission to promulgate the Guidelines, which would become binding on sentencing judges with very few exceptions.[42] And the SRA provided the government and defendants the right to appeal a sentence on the basis that the judge did not comply with the Guidelines.[43]

The first iteration of the Guidelines promulgated by the Commission went into effect on November 1, 1987. The centerpiece of the Guidelines is the Sentencing Table, a grid consisting of 258 different sentencing ranges.[44] The Sentencing Table's horizontal axis tracks the defendant's "Criminal History Category," which is adjusted based on his criminal history as defined in the Guidelines.[45] A defendant's criminal history category can range from I to VI.[46] The vertical axis tracks "Offense Level," which is determined by starting with a "base offense level" for the crime committed and then adjusting for a variety of "specific offense characteristics" that the Guidelines deems relevant, and may be between one and forty-three points.[47] The portion of the Sentencing Table where the defendant's criminal history category and offense level intersect represents the defendant's Guidelines sentencing range.[48] That range is quite narrow: its maximum "cannot exceed the minimum by more than the greater of" either twenty-five percent or six months.[49]

Under the pre-*Booker* Guidelines, the vast majority of sentences imposed fell within the Guidelines range.[50] But even before *Booker*, there were two means by which a judge could impose a sentence outside that range.[51] First, a court could impose a non-Guidelines sentence if "the court finds that there exists an aggravating or mitigating circumstance of a kind, or to a degree, not adequately taken into consideration by the Sentencing Commission . . . ."[52] I refer to these sentences as "Guidelines-sanctioned departures." Before *Booker*, Guidelines-sanctioned departures were almost always departures below the Guidelines range, and they "occurred in fewer than 10 percent of cases" nationwide.[53] The second, more common route of departure occurred when prosecutors filed a "substantial assistance motion" pursuant to section 5K1.1 of the Guidelines. The government may file such a motion, which "stat[es] that the defendant has provided substantial assistance in the investigation or prosecution of another person who has committed an offense," and which authorizes judges to depart from the Guidelines sentencing range.[54] During the period when the Guidelines were "mandatory," courts imposed such departures in fifteen to twenty percent of cases nationwide.[55]

While some prominent scholars argue that Congress did notintend for the SRA to eliminate judges' discretion to impose individualized sentences,[56] the Supreme Court disagreed. This more restrictive reading of the SRA contemplated a "mandatory" sentencing regime with minimal judicial discretion to depart from the Guidelines. In 1992, the Supreme Court held in *Williams v. United States* that a court's use of a ground for departure that was prohibited by the Guidelines' "policy statements" was an incorrect application of the Guidelines and constituted reversible error.[57] One year later, the Court held that the Guidelines' policy statements were binding on federal courts, and that the Commission's commentary must be "given controlling weight unless it is plainly erroneous or inconsistent with the [statute]."[58] Thus, before *Booker*, sentencing judges' ability to depart from the Guidelines-calculated sentence was quite limited.[59]

B. Booker and Its Progeny: A Return to Judicial Discretion in Sentencing

A series of decisions on the constitutionality of the Guidelines culminated in 2005 with *Booker*.[60] In *Booker*, the Court invalidated the provisions of the SRA that made the Guidelines mandatory.[61] The Court found the binding Guidelines scheme unconstitutional because it increased sentences on the basis of judicial fact finding rather than fact finding by a jury. The fix, the Court concluded, was simply to render the Guidelines advisory.

Since *Booker*, federal judges must begin by accurately calculating the Guidelines sentencing range, but may choose to depart from that range. The Court later clarified in *Gall v. United States* that the standard of review for such sentences is reasonableness, meaning abuse of discretion, regardless of whether the sentence falls within or outside the Guidelines range.[62] If the judge imposes a non-Guidelines sentence, the reasonableness standard applies regardless of the extent to which that sentence departs from the Guidelines range.[63] Appellate courts may apply a rebuttable presumption of reasonableness to Guidelines sentences,[64] but may not apply a presumption of unreasonableness to non-Guidelines sentences.[65]

While the sentencing judge must always use the correctly calculated Guidelines range as her starting point, she may impose a non-Guidelines sentence if she finds that deviating is necessary to "impose a sentence sufficient, but not greater than necessary" to comply with the sentencing factors set out in 18 U.S.C. § 3553(a), discussed in Section I.A.[66] The Court's "resounding overall message [post-*Booker*]is clear: *Booker* did indeed transform the Federal Sentencing Guidelines from 'law' to a lesser species, a form of quasi-law. Using the Court's terminology, the Guidelines are 'advice' that yield sentences that . . . can in most cases be judged 'reasonable.'"[67]

Perhaps unsurprisingly, the percentage of non-Guidelines sentences imposed has increased in the wake of *Booker* and its progeny.

After *Booker*, the percentage of cases in which judges imposed a Guidelines sentence fell consistently, while the percentage of non-government-sponsored below-range sentences steadily increased. By 2012, the percentage of "within-range" Guidelines sentences had fallen to just over 52%.[68]

C. The Economic Loss Table

As discussed in Section I.A, judges calculate a defendant's Guidelines sentencing range by first determining the defendant's criminal history category and the applicable offense level, and then identifying the relevant sentencing range from the Sentencing Table.[69] The base offense level for most economic crimes, such as larceny and fraud, is either six or seven levels.[70] The Guidelines include a multitude of factors that can result in enhancements to the offense level for these crimes. For instance, if the offense involved ten or more victims, two levels are added; if the offense involved receiving stolen property, and the defendant was a person in the business of receiving and selling stolen property, two levels are added; if the offense involved "a misrepresentation that the defendant was acting on behalf of a [religious] organization," two levels are added.[71]

Still other enhancements are transsubstantive in that they apply across all types of offenses—not just the financial crimes covered by section 2B1.1. For instance, if the defendant was an "organizer or leader of criminal activity that involved five or more participants," four levels are added.[72] The most significant of these transsubstantive enhancements is the concept of "relevant conduct," explained in the commentary of section 1B1.1 of the Guidelines. The definition of "offense" includes "the offense of conviction and all relevant conduct under section 1B1.3."[73] Under section 1B1.3, "relevant conduct" includes not just the defendant's offense of conviction, but all criminal activity that "occurred during the commission of the offense of conviction, in preparation for that offense, or in the course of attempting to avoid detection or responsibility for that offense."[74] When a judge determines whether a particular enhancement should apply, then, she must consider not only conduct related to the defendant's offense of conviction, but also any criminal conduct not charged—even criminal conduct of which the defendant was acquitted—if she determines by a preponderance of the evidence that such conduct occurred.[75] The Guidelines also import the Pinkerton doctrine for sentencing purposes[76]: the relevant conduct provision makes the defendant responsible for all crimes of his coconspirators if those acts were "reasonably foreseeable" to him.[77]

By far the most severe enhancement applicable to white-collar offenders is section 2B1.1(b), also known as the loss table, which provides offense level enhancements on the basis of the amount of loss attributed to the defendant. For example, if the loss exceeded

$30,000, six levels are added; if the loss exceeded $2,500,000, eighteen levels are added.[78] The rationale behind the loss table enhancements is simple: as the amount of economic loss caused by the defendant's crime increases, so does the seriousness of the crime and the defendant's culpability.

But the loss table frequently produces arbitrary and unduly severe sentences for two related reasons. First, the loss attributable to the defendant is defined so broadly that it can produce lifelong sentencing ranges for defendants who neither cause much economic harm nor derive much economic benefit from their crimes. Amendments made to the Guidelines in 2001[79] modified the relevant definition of "loss," which is now defined as the "reasonably foreseeable pecuniary harm that resulted from the offense."[80] Pecuniary harm, in turn, is the greater of the "actual loss" or the "intended loss" (the harm that was intended to result from the offense).[81]

Consider a defendant who intended to cause a loss of $1.5 million, but whose conduct did not cause any loss at all. He could receive the same enhancement—sixteen levels— as a defendant whose conduct actually resulted in a loss of $1.5 million.[82] The actual loss includes all "reasonably foreseeable pecuniary harm," or the harm "that the defendant knew or, under the circumstances, reasonably should have known, was a potential result of the offense."[83] So the amount of loss attributed to the defendant could either be a real amount (the actual loss) or a hypothetical amount (the intended loss), and may or may not have been foreseen by the defendant. Finally, the relevant loss could accrue to almost any individual or entity, or any group of individuals or entities, including the government and financial institutions.[84] For example, the amount ultimately attributed to Olis was $79 million, which was the loss in tax revenue to the United States Treasury that he intended to cause.[85] The way that "loss" is calculated under the Guidelines—by aggregating the total amount of loss caused (or intended to be caused) to any victim of the offense, and attributing that entire loss amount to the defendant and any co-conspirators—ensures that many defendants subject to loss table enhancements will receive extremely harsh Guidelines sentences. As the Second Circuit noted, "[I]t may well be that all but the most trivial frauds in publicly traded companies may trigger [Guidelines] sentences amounting to life imprisonment."[86]

Second, the loss table's enhancements are so large that, in practice, they dwarf other potentially more relevant considerations. The loss table provides for enhancements ranging from two levels (for a loss of more than $5,000) to thirty levels (for a loss of more than $400 million).[87] In contrast, an "organizer or leader of a criminal activity involving five or more participants" receives only a four-level enhancement and a "manager or supervisor" of the criminal activity receives a three-level enhancement, while a "minimal" participant receives a four-level reduction and a "minor" participant receives a two-level reduction.[88] The loss table enhancements can overwhelm other factors that are arguably more relevant to the defendant's culpability, including his role in the offense, his criminal history, and the economic benefit he received.

D. The 2015 Amendments

In addition to promulgating the Guidelines, policy statements, and official commentary, the Commission periodically reviews and proposes amendments to the Guidelines to Congress. On November 1, 2015, a new round of amendments took effect, several of which implicate white-collar sentencing.[89]

One change clarified the term "intended loss" by changing the definition from "the pecuniary harm that was intended to result from the offense" to "the pecuniary harm that the defendant purposely sought to inflict."[90] This amendment settled a circuit split over whether a subjective or objective test should be applied when calculating intended loss,[91] favoring the subjective test.[92] The Commission explained that this amendment "recognizes that sentencing enhancements predicated on intended loss, rather than losses that have actually accrued, should focus more specifically on the defendant's culpability."[93] Note, however, that this amendment does not affect how severely intended loss, as opposed to actual loss, is punished. As long as the defendant purposely sought to inflict a particular amount of pecuniary harm, he will receive the same enhancement under the loss table as a defendant who actually caused such losses to accrue. And intended loss still "includes intended pecuniary harm that would have been impossible or unlikely to occur."[94]

E. Gaps in the Literature on White-Collar Sentencing

The existing literature acknowledges that the Guidelines can produce extraordinarily high sentences for white-collar offenders. In particular, scholars have criticized the Guidelines's emphasis on economic loss for producing sentences that fail to capture a defendant's true culpability.[95] In criticizing the Guidelines, authors tend to focus on particular high-profile white-collar cases in which defendants received extraordinary sentences as examples "that should cause the Sentencing Commission and Congress to rethink the fraud Guidelines."[96] As Daniel Richman noted, "[P]erhaps because finding a useful quantitative metric is difficult, or because stable patterns have yet to emerge, assessments of the new regime have largely been driven by anecdote and rhetoric."[97] Moreover, much of the criticism of the white-collar Guidelines regime assumes that Guidelines sentences are actually imposed in most cases.[98] To the extent that the literature recognizes the discretion afforded by *Booker*,[99] some scholars assume this discretion will have a limited effect in the area of white-collar crime; others see increased discretion as particularly well-suited to white-collar cases.[100] While some scholarship considers whether judges should use their post-*Booker* discretion to impose below-range sentences in major white-collar cases, the literature thus far has not considered the extent to which judges actually mitigate the effects of the Guidelines in major white-collar cases by imposing below-range sentences. In particular, no empirical study has explained (1) how often judges impose below-range sentences in major white-collar cases; or

(2) when such sentences are imposed, the extent to which those sentences are shorter than the Guidelines sentencing range. This Note seeks to fill that gap.

Endnotes

36. 36. See DANIEL C. RICHMAN ET AL., DEFINING FEDERAL CRIMES 661 (2014).

37. See id.

38. See S. REP. NO. 98-225, at 38-65 (1983).

39. KATE STITH & JOSÉ A. CABRANES, FEAR OF JUDGING: SENTENCING GUIDELINES IN THE FEDERAL COURTS 36 (1998) (quoting MARVIN E. FRANKEL, CRIMINAL SENTENCES: LAW WITHOUT ORDER 119 (1973)).

40. FRANKEL, CRIMINAL SENTENCES, supra note 39, at 113.

41. Id. Frankel's book focused almost exclusively on the problem of sentencing disparities rather than on the problem of too harsh (or too lenient) sentences. In fact, a series of compromises made in order to garner Republican support resulted in a provision of the SRA that directed the Commission to increase penalties for violent and white-collar crimes. See RICHMAN ET AL., supra note 36, at 669; STITH & CABRANES, supra note 39, at 39-48.

42. See STITH & CABRANES, supra note 39, at 1-2.

43. See S. REP. NO. 98-225, at 51-52.

44. See U.S. SENT'G COMMISSION, supra note 11.

45. See U.S. SENTENCING GUIDELINES MANUAL § 1B1.1(a)(6) (U.S. SENTENCING COMM'N 2014).

46. See U.S. SENT'G COMMISSION, supra note 11.

47. See U.S. SENTENCING GUIDELINES MANUAL § 1B1.1(a)(2)-(4) (U.S. SENTENCING COMM'N 2014); U.S. SENT'G COMMISSION, supra note 11.

48. See U.S. SENTENCING GUIDELINES MANUAL § 1B1.1(a) (U.S. SENTENCING COMM'N 2014).

49. Id. ch. 1, pt. A(1)(4)(h).

50. For instance, in 2002, 74.5% of all sentences imposed were within the Guidelines range in S.D.N.Y. 2002 Sourcebook of Federal Sentencing Statistics, U.S. SENT'G COMMISSION 53 tbl.26 (2002), http://www.ussc.gov/sites/default/files/pdf/research-and-publications/annual-reports-and-sourcebooks/2002/table26.pdf [http://perma.cc/QP G9-ZUH3].

51. In this Note, I use the term "non-Guidelines sentence" to refer to any sentence imposed that is not within the Guidelines-calculated range as determined by the sentencing judge. A nonGuidelines sentence could either exceed or fall short of the Guidelines sentencing range.

52. 18 U.S.C. § 3553(b)(1) (2012).

53. See RICHMAN ET AL., supra note 36, at 670.

54. U.S. SENTENCING GUIDELINES MANUAL § 5K1.1 (U.S. SENTENCING COMM'N 2014). While these kinds of sentences are "government-sponsored," the judge still decides the length of each defendant's sentence.

55. See RICHMAN ET AL., supra note 36, at 670.

56. Amy Baron-Evans and Kate Stith argue that rather than significantly restricting judges' sentencing discretion, the SRA anticipated that judges would retain broad authority to depart from the Guidelines: The judge would first consider the nature and circumstances of the offense, the history and characteristics of the defendant, and the purposes of sentencing, as required by § 3553(a). This consideration would inform the judge's decision as to whether the guideline range adequately reflected the circumstances of the case and whether a different sentence should result, as required by § 3553(b). The judge would then determine the guideline range, and either sentence within the guideline range because it appropriately reflected the relevant factors, or sentence outside the guideline range because it did not. Amy Baron-Evans & Kate Stith, Booker Rules, 160 U. PA. L. REV. 1631, 1647-48 (2012) (emphasis omitted) (footnotes omitted).

57. 503 U.S. 193, 200 (1992).

58. *Stinson v. United States*, 508 U.S. 36, 45 (1993) (quoting *Bowles v. Seminole Rock & Sand Co.*, 325 U.S. 410, 414 (1945)). In addition to the Guidelines, Congress authorized the Commission to promulgate "policy statements" regarding, among other things, the "application of the guidelines or any other aspect of sentencing." 28 U.S.C. § 994(a)(2) (2012).

59. Although, as discussed, limited means of departing from the Guidelines sentencing range were available prior to *Booker*, for convenience I refer to the pre-*Booker* regime as "mandatory."

60. 543 U.S. 220 (2005).

61. Id. at 227; see also *Blakely v. Washington*, 542 U.S. 296, 312-14 (2004) (holding Washington State's sentencing-guideline system unconstitutional and requiring proof beyond a reasonable doubt for any fact (other than the fact of a prior conviction or one admitted by the defendant) that increases the penalty beyond the statutory maximum); *Apprendi v. New Jersey*, 530 U.S. 466, 497 (2000) (holding five-four that a statutory hate crime enhancement that increased the statutory maximum was functionally equivalent to an element of a greater offense and, therefore, facts establishing a hate crime should have been submitted to the jury).

62. 552 U.S. 38, 51 (2007).

63. Id. at 47 ("We reject, however, an appellate rule that requires 'extraordinary' circumstances to justify a sentence outside the Guidelines range. We also reject the use of a rigid mathematical formula that uses the percentage of a departure as the standard for determining the strength of the justifications required for a specific sentence.").

64. See *Rita v. United States*, 551 U.S. 338, 347 (2007).

65. See Gall, 552 U.S. at 47.

66. 18 U.S.C. § 3553(a) (2012); see also *Kimbrough v. United States*, 552 U.S. 85, 109 (2007) (discussing the sentencing judge's role in weighing § 3553(a) factors to reach a nonGuidelines sentence).

67. Kate Stith, The Arc of the Pendulum: Judges, Prosecutors, and the Exercise of Discretion, 117 YALE L.J. 1420, 1492 (2008).

68. See Figure 1.

69. See supra notes 44-49 and accompanying text.

70. U.S. SENTENCING GUIDELINES MANUAL § 2B1.1(a) (U.S. SENTENCING COMM'N 2014).

71. Id. § 2B1.1(b)(2)(B), (b)(4), (b)(9).

72. Id. § 3B1.1(a).

73. Id. § 1B1.1 cmt. 1(H) (emphasis added). For background on the relevant conduct provision of the Guidelines, see William W. Wilkins, Jr. & John R. Steer, Relevant Conduct: The Cornerstone of the Federal Sentencing Guidelines, 41 S.C. L. REV. 495 (1990).

74. U.S. SENTENCING GUIDELINES MANUAL § 1B1.3(a)(1) (U.S. SENTENCING COMM'N 2014).

75. See United States v. Watts, 519 U.S. 148, 148 (1997) (holding that a defendant convicted of possessing cocaine base with intent to distribute, but acquitted of using a firearm in relation to a drug offense, may still be given a higher sentence where the sentencing judge found by a preponderance of the evidence that the defendant in fact possessed the gun).

76. See Pinkerton v. United States, 328 U.S. 640, 647-48 (1946). Consider, for example, a defendant whom prosecutors charge as a co-conspirator in a drug conspiracy. Say the jury acquits the defendant on the conspiracy charge: that is, the jury refuses to make the defendant criminally liable for crimes committed by others in the conspiracy. Even in this circumstance, the sentencing judge would be required by the Guidelines to attribute those other crimes to the defendant if the judge found by a preponderance of the evidence that the co-conspirators' criminal activity was in fact reasonably foreseeable to the defendant.

77. U.S. SENTENCING GUIDELINES MANUAL § 1B1.3(a)(1)(B) (U.S. SENTENCING COMM'N 2014).

78. Id. § 2B1.1(b)(1)(D), (J). On November 1, 2015, a round of amendments to the loss table took effect, slightly altering the amount of loss that triggers each enhancement. For instance, the amount of loss that triggers a 2-level enhancement increased from more than $5,000 to more than $6,500. These amendments are meant to account for inflation. See U.S. SENT'G COMMISSION, supra note 35, at 15-24.

79. See Amendments to the Sentencing Guidelines, U.S. SENT'G COMMISSION 19-90 (2001), http://www.ussc.gov/sites/default/files/pdf/amendment-process/reader-friendly-amendments/20010501_RF_Amendments.pdf [http://perma.cc/79HW-9PRU].

80. U.S. SENTENCING GUIDELINES MANUAL § 2B1.1 cmt. n.3 (U.S. SENTENCING COMM'N 2014); see also Office of Gen. Counsel, Loss Primer (§2B1.1(b)(1)), U.S. SENT'G COMMISSION 1 (2013), http://www.ussc.gov/Legal/Primers/Primer_Loss.pdf [http://perma.cc/2LQF5EMW] (noting that the Commission "modified the definition of loss such that it would be based on reasonably foreseeable pecuniary harm and would include intended loss").

81. U.S. SENTENCING GUIDELINES MANUAL § 2B1.1 cmt. n.3 (U.S. SENTENCING COMM'N 2014).

82. See id. § 2B1.1(b)(1).

83. Id. § 2B1.1 cmt. n.3 (emphasis added).

84. See id. § 2B1.1(b).

85. See Olis II, No. H-03-217-01, 2006 WL 2716048, at *10 (S.D. Tex. Sept. 22, 2006).

86. *United States v. Ebbers*, 458 F.3d 110, 129 (2d Cir. 2006).

87. U.S. SENTENCING GUIDELINES MANUAL § 2B1.1(b) (U.S. SENTENCING COMM'N 2014)

88. Id. § 3B1.1-2.

89. See U.S. SENT'G COMMISSION, supra note 35, at 1.

90. Id. at 28.

91. Compare, e.g., *United States v. Manatau*, 647 F.3d 1048, 1048 (10th Cir. 2011) (holding that a subjective inquiry into the defendant's purpose is required), with *United States v. Innarelli*, 524 F.3d 286, 291 (1st Cir. 2008) (holding that the loss inquiry should be guided by the objectively reasonable expectations of a person in the defendant's position).

92. See U.S. SENT'G COMMISSION, supra note 35, at 29.

93. Id.

94. U.S. SENTENCING GUIDELINES MANUAL § 2B1.1 cmt. n.3 (U.S. SENTENCING COMM'N 2014); see U.S. SENT'G COMMISSION, supra note 35, at 29 (omitting any changes to the definition of intended loss that would alter this inclusion). Another amendment adds an enhancement of between 2 and 6 levels based on "substantial financial hardship" to a designated number of victims ranging from 1 or more (2 levels) to 25 or more (6 levels). U.S. SENT'G COMMISSION, supra note 35, at 26. These enhancements replace those previously applied based on the total number of victims of the offense without consideration for the hardship suffered by such victims. Id. The 2015 Amendments also alter the way that loss is calculated in cases involving fraudulent manipulation of value of a publicly traded security or commodity by removing the rebuttable presumption in favor of applying the "fraud on the market" theory. Under this amendment, courts are free to "use any method that is appropriate and practicable under the circumstances." Id. at 30. Finally, the 2015 Amendments change the enhancement applicable to "sophisticated means." Id. at 29. The enhancement applicable on the basis of the use of "sophisticated means" will now apply only if the defendant's own conduct was sophisticated—not where the offense itself involved sophisticated means. Id.

95. See, e.g., Derick R. Vollrath, Note, Losing the Loss Calculation: Toward a More Just Sentencing Regime in White-Collar Criminal Cases, 59 DUKE L.J. 1001, 1001 (2010) ("The U.S. Sentencing Guidelines recommend sentences that are generally too high and place a grossly disproportionate emphasis on the concept of 'loss' . . . . This concept of loss is ill defined, and often artificial to the point of being arbitrary. Moreover, the loss calculation fails to adequately approximate a defendant's culpability, dwarfing traditionally relevant considerations such as the manner in which the defendant committed the crime and the defendant's motive for doing so.").

96. Weissmann & Block, supra note 33, at 291; see also, e.g., Podgor, supra note 33, at 279-81 (characterizing the sentences imposed on Bernie Ebbers, John Rigas, Timothy Rigas, and Jeff Skilling as examples of the deficiency of the current white-collar sentencing regime).

97. Daniel Richman, Federal White Collar Sentencing in the United States: A Work in Progress, 76 LAW & CONTEMP. PROBS. 53, 60 (2013).

98. See, e.g., Ellen S. Podgor, The Challenge of White Collar Sentencing, 97 J. CRIM. L. & CRIMINOLOGY 731, 731-32 (2007) ("White collar offenders have faced sentences far beyond those imposed in prior years. . . . Although the sentencing guidelines have

some flexibility resulting from the recent Supreme Court decision in *United States v. Booker*, the culture of mandated guidelines still permeates the structure and, as such, prominently advises the judiciary." (citations omitted)); see also Vollrath, supra note 95, at 1003 ("Despite [their] flaws, the Guidelines continue to dominate sentencing. Although the Supreme Court rendered the Guidelines no longer mandatory in *United States v. Booker*, judges still adhere to the Guidelines with roughly the same frequency as before the *Booker* decision. A culture of mandated guidelines continues to permeate the federal sentencing regime." (citations omitted)).

99. Baron-Evans and Stith offer a comprehensive account of the effects of *Booker* and its progeny, arguing that *Booker* provided the "fix" necessary to change the sentencing process for the better by allowing a return to individualized sentencing that considers "all relevant facts about the offense and the offender." Baron-Evans & Stith, supra note 56, at 1742.

100. Compare Daniel A. Chatham, Note, Playing with Post-*Booker* Fire: The Dangers of Increased Judicial Discretion in Federal White Collar Sentencing, 32 J. CORP. L. 619, 627 (2007) ("[I]t is probable that most of the downward departures have come in drug cases, as the drug guidelines are much higher than white collar guidelines and are more universally decried by district court judges."), with Vollrath, supra note 95, at 1005 (arguing that the increased discretion afforded to judges by *Kimbrough v. United States* "can and should apply to the sentencing of white-collar criminals, allowing judges to move away from the Sentencing Guidelines' disproportionate emphasis on loss").

> "Our democratically elected
> parliamentarians have the duty to
> establish sentencing benchmarks that
> they believe reflect national values
> on how different crimes should
> be punished."

Mandatory Minimum Sentences Deliver Clarity to a Sometimes Muddled Sentencing System

David Butt

In the following viewpoint, David Butt argues that democratically-elected legislators have the responsibility and the duty to establish mandatory sentencing minimums that they believe reflect the values of society. But, the author contends, many mandatory minimum sentences have "Run afoul of our Charter of Rights," and with a modest tweak to Parliament's current approach, all these polarizing clashes could have been avoided. The author believes that a simple fix to the problem would be to enact presumptive minimum sentences by writing laws so the convicted criminal will receive the prescribed mandatory penalty: With a modest tweak to Parliament's current approach, all these polarizing clashes could have been avoided. David Butt is a Toronto-based criminal lawyer.

"In the Real World, Mandatory Minimum Sentencing Works Just Fine," by David Butt, *The Globe and Mail* (Toronto), October 7, 2015. Reprinted by permission.

As you read, consider the following questions:

1. What do democratically elected parliamentarians have the duty to establish?
2. What has experience taught us about a tiny minority of cases, according to the viewpoint author?
3. What does the viewpoint author suggest as a fix to this polarizing problem?

Last week, yet another mandatory minimum sentence bit the dust. An Ontario Superior Court judge, Bruce Durno, a judge with an impeccable pedigree in criminal law stretching back for decades, and a judge widely acknowledged within the profession as scrupulously fair-minded, said the mandatory minimum sentence for growing more than six marijuana plants could be cruel and unusual punishment, so down it went.

The pot plant mandatory minimum falls into what is now an embarrassingly crowded trash bin of similar minimum sentences that have run afoul of our Charter of Rights. But it didn't have to be this way. With a modest tweak to Parliament's current approach, all these polarizing clashes could have been avoided.

In an election season it is tempting to frame the debate about mandatory minimum sentences in political terms. The right-leaning political argument is that unelected, soft-on-crime judges are thwarting the will of a democratically elected Parliament taking a strong stand against serious offenders. The left-leaning political argument is that compassion and sensitivity to personal circumstances, so essential to a just sentence, are cruelly eliminated from the balance by mandatory minimum sentences.

Both of these arguments are caricatures that misrepresent a much more nuanced and apolitical reality that all professional participants in the criminal justice system face every day.

On the one hand, certainty in sentencing has benefits that have nothing to do with right-leaning political beliefs. Long before mandatory minimum sentencing escalated in prominence, the courts themselves fostered a deep tradition of sentencing ranges or tariffs for particular crimes, and insisted that those tariffs be applied consistently. Even without mandatory minimums, every good criminal lawyer and judge knew with reasonable certainty the going rate for a particular crime. So discussions and arguments about what sentence to pass were always premised on the going rate. Disagreement between the prosecution and defense was almost always within a responsibly constrained range of options, and the vast majority of criminal cases settled by agreement.

On the other hand, experience has repeatedly taught that there is always a tiny minority of cases that are truly statistical outliers. The facts of these rare cases are so unusual, sometimes so bizarre, that they cry out for differential treatment, for departure from the prevailing tariff. These outlier cases are by no means common. They do not undermine the wisdom of the prevailing tariff for that particular crime. Indeed they are the exceptions that by their uniqueness actually demonstrate the wisdom of the prevailing tariff. Treating these outlier cases differently has nothing to do with softness or left-leaning political beliefs, and everything to do with simply recognizing a statistical anomaly for what it is.

Our democratically elected parliamentarians have the duty to establish sentencing benchmarks that they believe reflect national values on how different crimes should be punished. And again, contrary to some of the less responsible political rhetoric, judges have a long and proud tradition of thoughtfully implementing, not thwarting, the will of Parliament. So there is nothing at all problematic in principle with Parliament passing and judges imposing mandatory minimum sentences. That is not the only way to approach sentencing, but it is certainly an available legislative option. Mandatory minimum sentences deliver clarity to a sentencing system in which, generally speaking, clarity is a virtue.

The problem arises when Parliament ignores the inevitability of the statistical outlier, the rare case that truly cannot fit the mold of a mandatory minimum sentence. In these rare cases, the mandatory minimum would be grossly disproportionate and therefore cruel. Faced with such a statistical outlier case, the judge has no choice but to strike down the entire mandatory minimum scheme. So a mandatory minimum sentence that works just fine in the overwhelming majority of cases will be struck down because we quite rightly refuse to tolerate a cruel law, even if it is cruel only rarely. When it comes to striking down mandatory minimum sentences, the tail wags the dog.

The fix to this polarizing problem is simple. Enact presumptive minimum sentences: Write the law so that the convicted criminal will receive the prescribed mandatory penalty, unless he or she demonstrates that his or her case is so unique that the mandatory penalty would be grossly disproportionate. A presumptive minimum sentence is a mandatory minimum with a narrow escape clause. Other jurisdictions use precisely this tool. A presumptive minimum sentence delivers the certainty and moral clarity that make mandatory minimum sentences attractive. And the narrow escape clause in the presumptive minimum sentence delivers the flexibility actually needed to address rare statistical outliers.

And the tail will no longer wag the dog.

Periodical and Internet Sources Bibliography

The following articles have been selected to supplement the diverse views presented in this chapter.

Matthew Beaton, "Lawmakers Re-Examine Mandatory Minimums," *News Herald* (Panama City, FL). March 13, 2013. http://www .newsherald.com/article/20130312/news/303129978.

"EDITORIAL: Leave Sentencing Decision to Those Who Know Best," *Pantagraph* (Bloomington, IL), March 27, 2013.

FDL News, Department of Justice Memo on Savings to Taxpayers from Passage of the Smarter Sentencing Act, July 25, 2015, http:// news.firedoglake.com/department-of-justice-memo-on-savings-to-taxpayers-from-passage-of-the-smarter-sentencing-act/.

Sylvia Hsieh, "Sentencing Ruling by U.S. Supreme Court Affects Drug and Gun Cases," *Lawyers USA*, June 19, 2013.

Rachel Martin, "Former Prosecutor on Why He Supports Mandatory Minimums," Morning Edition (NPR), May 31, 2017. https://www. npr.org/2017/05/31/530843623/former-prosecutor-on-why-he -supports-mandatory-minimums.

"Prosecuting Prosecutors for Intentional Misconduct," More Content Now, *Daily Record* (Rochester, NY), August 15, 2016.

Emma M. Quinn-Judge and Monica R. Shah, "With 'Laltaprasad' Case, SJC on Verge of 'Momentous Decision'," *Massachusetts Lawyers Weekly*, April 1, 2016. http://masslawyersweekly .com/2016/04/01/with-laltaprasad-case-sjc-on-verge-of-momentous-decision/.

David Sheff, "Trump's War on Drug Users," *USA Today*, May 10, 2017. https://www.usatoday.com/story/opinion/2017/05/05/trump-war-drug-mental-health-reform-column/101252422/.

April M. Short, "6 Shocking Revelations About How Private Prisons Make Their Money," Alternet, September 20, 2013. https://www .alternet.org/civil-liberties/6-shocking-revelations-about-how -private-prisons-make-their-money.

Hedy Weinberg , "Congratulations! The Taxes You Just Paid Might Be on Their Way to a Private Prison," ACLU, April 15, 2014. https:// www.aclu.org/blog/congratulations-taxes-you-just-paid-might-be-their-way-private-prison.

CHAPTER 3

Do Mandatory Minimum Sentences Reflect Ethnic or Racial Bias?

Chapter Preface

In reaction to an increase in the amount of cocaine being smuggled into the United States and the cocaine epidemic in the 1980s, the US Congress and many state legislatures adopted laws that stiffened the penalties for anyone convicted of trafficking certain illegal drugs. As a result, jail terms became mandatory for drug dealers and anybody possessing certain amounts of illegal drugs. While many Americans support these laws, some view them as inherently biased and discriminatory against African Americans.

One example was that possession of powdered cocaine, a drug associated with affluent white businessmen, was sentenced less severely than possession of crack cocaine, a drug associated with inner-city African American men. A person convicted of possessing 500 grams (one-half kilogram) or more of powdered cocaine will be sentenced to five years in prison with no possibility of parole. In comparison, just five grams of crack cocaine qualifies for the five-year mandatory term, and this increases to ten years for 50 grams of crack. According to the US Sentencing Commission, in the federal justice system, mandatory minimum provisions for drug-related activities carry penalties ranging from five years to life.

Punishing these criminals with very harsh prison terms was at first regarded as too severe, at least for those who were cocaine users and small-time dealers. But here the issue of race as the "demonizer" enters into the lawmaking equation. Crack cocaine was disproportionately sold and used in minority neighborhoods, while a higher percentage of white suburbanites favored the powdered form. Critics of the federal mandatory sentencing drug laws claim that the severely stricter penalties for using and dealing crack cocaine versus cocaine in its powered form—a defendant must have possessed one hundred times more powder than crack to be eligible for the five-year or the ten-year mandatory sentence—are correlated with probabilities that an arrested dealer or user will be a member of a racial minority.

> *"Evidence suggests that some individuals are incarcerated not solely because of their crime, but because of racially disparate policies, beliefs, and practices, rendering these collateral consequences all the more troubling."*

Mandatory Minimum Sentencing Has Resulted in a Disproportionate African American Prison Population

Ashley Nellis

In the following excerpted viewpoint, Ashley Nellis argues that African Americans are incarcerated in state prisons across the country at more than five times the rate of whites in many states, and at least ten times the rate in five states. The author documents the rates of incarceration for whites, African Americans, and Hispanics in each state, identifies three contributors to racial and ethnic disparities in imprisonment, and provides recommendations for reform. Dr. Ashley Nellis has an academic and professional background in analyzing criminal justice policies and practices, and has extensive experience in studying racial and ethnic disparities in the justice system.

"The Color of Justice: Racial and Ethnic Disparity in State Prisons," by Ashley Nellis, The Sentencing Project, June 14, 2016. Reprinted by permission.

As you read, consider the following questions:

1. What are the key findings of the report used in the viewpoint?
2. What disparities need to be acknowledged before the criminal justice system can be reformed in a meaningful way?
3. What is driving the disparity regarding racial and ethnic populations in prisons?

Truly meaningful reforms to the criminal justice system cannot be accomplished without acknowledgement of racial and ethnic disparities in the prison system, and focused attention on reduction of disparities. Since the majority of people in prison are sentenced at the state level rather than the federal level, it is critical to understand the variation in racial and ethnic composition across states, and the policies and the day-to-day practices that contribute to this variance.[4] Incarceration creates a host of collateral consequences that include restricted employment prospects, housing instability, family disruption, stigma, and disenfranchisement. These consequences set individuals back by imposing new punishments after prison. Collateral consequences are felt disproportionately by people of color, and because of concentrations of poverty and imprisonment in certain jurisdictions, it is now the case that entire communities experience these negative effects.[5] Evidence suggests that some individuals are incarcerated not solely because of their crime, but because of racially disparate policies, beliefs, and practices, rendering these collateral consequences all the more troubling. An unwarranted level of incarceration that worsens racial disparities is problematic not only for the impacted group, but for society as whole, weakening the justice system's potential and undermining perceptions of justice.

[...]

Overall Findings

The Bureau of Justice Statistics reports that 35% of state prisoners are white, 38% are black, and 21% are Hispanic.[7] In twelve states more than half of the prison population is African American. Though the reliability of data on ethnicity is not as strong as it is for race estimates, the Hispanic population in state prisons is as high as 61% in New Mexico and 42% in both Arizona and California. In an additional seven states, at least one in five inmates is Hispanic.[8] While viewing percentages reveals a degree of disproportion for people of color when compared to the overall general population (where 62% are white, 13% are black, and 17% are Hispanic),[9] viewing the composition of prison populations from this perspective only tells some of the story. In this report we present the rates of racial and ethnic disparity, which allow a portrayal of the overrepresentation of people of color in the prison system accounting for population in the general community.[10] This shows odds of imprisonment for individuals in various racial and ethnic categories.

It is important to note at the outset that, given the absence or unreliability of ethnicity data in some states, the racial/ethnic disparities in those states may be understated. Since most Hispanics in those instances would be counted in the white prison population, the white rate of incarceration would therefore appear higher than is the case, and consequently the black/white and Hispanic/white ratios of disparity would be lower as well. In four states, data on ethnicity is not reported to the Bureau of Justice Statistics, nor is it provided in the state department of corrections' individual annual reports. These states are Alabama, Maryland, Montana, and Vermont. There are most assuredly people in prison in these states who are Hispanic, but since the state does not record this information, the exact number is unknown.

[…]

The Scale of Disparity

The particular drivers of disparity may be related to policy, offending, implicit bias, or some combination. Regardless of the causes, however, the simple fact of these disparities should be disturbing given the consequences for individuals and communities. One has to wonder whether there would have been more of an urgency to understand and remedy the disparity directly had the ratios been reversed. While chronic racial and ethnic disparity in imprisonment has been a known feature of the prison system for many decades,[11] there has been relatively little serious consideration of adjustments that can be made—inside or outside the justice system—toward changing this pattern.

Racial disparities in incarceration can arise from a variety of circumstances. These might include a high rate of black incarceration, a low rate of white incarceration, or varying combinations. We note that the states with the highest ratio of disparity in imprisonment are generally those in the northeast or upper Midwest, while Southern states tend to have lower ratios. The low Southern ratios are generally produced as a result of high rates of incarceration for all racial groups. For example, Arkansas and Florida both have a black/white ratio of imprisonment considerably below the national average of 5.1:1 (3.8:1 and 3.6:1, respectively). Yet both states incarcerate African Americans at higher than average rates, 18% higher in Arkansas and 15% higher in Florida. But these rates are somewhat offset by the particularly high white rates, 61% higher than the national average in Arkansas and 63% higher in Florida.

Conversely, in the states with the highest degree of disparity, this is often produced by a higher than average black rate, but a relatively low white rate.[12]

The scale of racial disparity in incarceration can also be seen by comparing states that have lower than average black incarceration rates to those with higher than average white incarceration rates. Here we find that the states with the highest white incarceration rates (Oklahoma, Idaho, Texas, Florida, and Arizona) fall below the states with the lowest black rates (Hawaii, Massachusetts[13], Maine, Maryland, and North Dakota).

Drivers of Disparity

Persistent racial disparities have long been a focus in criminological research and the presence of disparities is not disputed.[14] Proposed explanations for disparities range from variations in offending based on race to biased decision-making in the criminal justice system, and also include a range of individual level factors such as poverty, education outcomes, unemployment history, and criminal history.[15] Research in this area finds a smaller amount of unwarranted disparity for serious crimes like homicide than for less serious crimes, especially drug crimes.

Alfred Blumstein's work in this area examined racial differences in arrests and, after comparing these to prison demographics, determined that approximately 80% of prison disparity among state prisoners in 1979 was explained by differential offending by race, leaving 20% unexplained. He noted that if there was no discrimination after arrest, the racial makeup of prisoners should approximate the population of arrestees. The greatest amount of unexplained disparity was found among drug offenses: nearly half of the racial disparity for prison among those convicted of drug crimes could not be explained by arrest. In a follow-up study, Blumstein found that the proportion of racial disparities found in prisons explained by arrests in 1991 had declined to 76%.[16] Subsequent studies have replicated this work with more recent data and found even higher amounts of unexplained disparities, particularly in the category of drug arrests.[17]

One issue raised by Blumstein's approach is that the use of arrest records as a reflection of criminal involvement may be more accurate for serious offenses than less serious offenses. For less serious crimes, authorities may exercise greater discretion at the point of arrest.[18] Cassia Spohn's research on sentencing reasons that for less serious crimes, judges might depart from the constraints of the law, allowing other factors to enter into their judgment. These factors might include forms of racial bias related to perceived racial threat.[19] Despite the possibility of failing to account for all variance, research that relies on incident reporting (i.e., self-report data rather than police data) to circumvent these potential problems also reveals unexplained racial disparities. Patrick Langan's work, for example, estimated unexplained disparity to be in the range of 15–16%, and though this is a smaller amount of unexplained variance (compared to that found by Blumstein, for example) it is likely due to the fact that his analysis did not include drug offenses.[20]

Analyses of more recent data all come to similar conclusions: a sizable proportion of racial disparities in prison cannot be explained by criminal offending.[21] Some analyses have focused on single states[22] while others have looked at all states individually to note the range of disparity.[23] Studies that examine regional differences within states are also revealing. Researchers Gaylen Armstrong and Nancy Rodriguez, whose work centers on county-level differences in juvenile justice outcomes found that it is not solely individual-level characteristics that influence outcomes, but the composition of the community where the juvenile resides that makes a difference as well. Specifically, they conclude that "juvenile delinquents who live within areas that have high minority populations (more heterogeneous) will more often be detained, regardless of their individual race or ethnicity."[24] And finally, studies seeking to better understand the processes between arrest and imprisonment, particularly at the stage of sentencing, have been pursued in order to better understand the unexplained disparities in state prisons.[25]

[...]

Policies and Practices

The criminal justice system is held together by policies and practices, both formal and informal, which influence the degree to which an individual penetrates the system. At multiple points in the system, race may play a role. Disparities mount as individuals

MASS INCARCERATION

With over two million people in prison, the United States incarcerates more people than any other nation. And a big driver of our mass incarceration are mandatory minimum sentencing requirements.

Before mandatory minimums became so prevalent, when a person was convicted of a crime, judges had a great deal of discretion in deciding a person's sentence. But in the 1980s and 90s, federal and state government passed laws requiring predetermined sentences for certain crimes. So whereas judges used to be able to consider the individual factors in each case to ensure a sentence made sense for each circumstance, mandatory minimums require judges to issue fixed, predetermined sentence lengths. Critics of these sentencing schemes refer to them as a cookie-cutter approach to justice.

These pre-determined sentences are called mandatory minimums. And they have wreaked havoc on Oregon and across the country.

"District Attorneys And Mandatory Minimums," They Report To You.

progress through the system, from the initial point of arrest to the final point of imprisonment.[26] Harsh punishment policies adopted in recent decades, some of which were put into effect even after the crime decline began, are the main cause of the historic rise in imprisonment that has occurred over the past 40 years.[27]

The rise in incarceration that has come to be known as mass imprisonment began in 1973 and can be attributed to three major eras of policymaking, all of which had a disparate impact on people of color, especially African Americans. Until 1986, a series of policies was enacted to expand the use of imprisonment for a variety of felonies. After this point, the focus moved to greater levels of imprisonment for drug and sex offenses. There was a particularly sharp growth in state imprisonment for drug offenses between 1987 and 1991. In the final stage, beginning around 1995, the emphasis was on increasing both prison likelihood and significantly lengthening prison sentences.[28]

Harsh drug laws are clearly an important factor in the persistent racial and ethnic disparities observed in state prisons. For drug crimes disparities are especially severe, due largely to the fact that blacks are nearly four times as likely as whites to be arrested for drug offenses and 2.5 times as likely to be arrested for drug possession.[29] This is despite the evidence that whites and blacks use drugs at roughly the same rate. From 1995 to 2005, African Americans comprised approximately 13 percent of drug users but 36% of drug arrests and 46% of those convicted for drug offenses.[30]

Disparities are evident at the initial point of contact with police, especially through policies that target specific areas and/or people. A popular example of this is "stop, question, and frisk." Broad discretion allowed to law enforcement can aggravate disparities. Though police stops alone are unlikely to result in a conviction that would lead to a prison sentence, the presence of a criminal record is associated with the decision to incarcerate for subsequent offenses, a sequence of events that disadvantages African Americans. Jeffrey Fagan's work in this area found that police officers' selection of who to stop in New York City's high-profile policing program was dictated more by racial composition of the neighborhood than by actual crime in the area.[31] The process of stopping, questioning and frisking individuals based on little more than suspicion (or on nebulous terms such as "furtive behavior," which were the justification for many stops) has led to unnecessary criminal records for thousands. New York's policy was ruled unconstitutional in 2013 with a court ruling in *Floyd v. City of New York*.

Other stages of the system contribute to the racial composition of state prisons as well. Factors such as pre-trial detention—more likely to be imposed on black defendants because of income inequality—contributes to disparities because those who are detained pre-trial are more likely to be convicted and sentenced to longer prison terms.[32] Cassia Spohn's analysis of 40 states' sentencing processes finds that, though crime seriousness and prior record are key determinants at sentencing, the non-legal factors of race and ethnicity also influence sentencing decisions. She notes that "black and Hispanic offenders—particularly those who are young, male, and unemployed—are more likely than their white counterparts to be sentenced to prison than similarly situated white offenders. Other categories of racial minorities—those convicted of drug offenses, those who victimize whites, those who accumulate more serious prior criminal records, or those who refuse to plead guilty or are unable to secure pretrial release—also may be singled out for more punitive treatment."[33]

Still other research finds that prosecutorial charging decisions play out unequally when viewed by race, placing blacks at a disadvantage to whites. Prosecutors are more likely to charge black defendants under state habitual offender laws than similarly situated white defendants.[34] Researchers in Florida found evidence for this relationship, and also observed that the relationship between race and use of the state habitual offender law was stronger for less serious crimes than it was for more serious crimes.[35] California's three strikes law has been accused of widening disparities because of the greater likelihood of prior convictions for African Americans.

[…]

Endnotes

4. Neill, K. A., Yusuf, J., & Morris, J.C. (2014). Explaining dimensions of state-level punitiveness in the United States: The roles of social, economic, and cultural factors. *Criminal Justice Policy Review* 26(2):751-772.

5. Clear, T., Rose, D., & Ryder, J. (2001). Incarceration and the community: The problem of removing and returning offenders. *Crime and Delinquency* 47(3): 335-351; Lynch, J. & Sabol, W. (2001). Prisoner reentry in perspective (Vol. 3, Crime Policy Report). Washington, DC: Urban Institute; National Research Council (2014). The growth of incarceration in the United States: exploring causes and consequences. Washington, DC: The National Academies Press.

7. Carson, E. A. (2015). Prisoners in 2014. Washington, DC: Bureau of Justice Statistics. Six percent of prisoners are composed of racial groups that fall under the category of "other."

8. Colorado, Connecticut, Massachusetts, Nevada, New York, Nevada, and Texas.

9. U.S. Census (2015). Quick facts: United States.

10. Though this report focuses on rates of disparity, it is still informative to view the composition of prisons as percentages. We have provided two tables that contain this information in Appendix A, Tables 1 & 2.

11. National Research Council (2014). The growth of incarceration in the United States: Exploring causes and consequences. Washington, DC: The National Academies Press.

12. This observation is documented elsewhere as well. See, for example, Blumstein, A. (1993). Racial disproportionality revisited. University of Colorado Law Review, 64: 743-760; Mauer, M. (1997). Intended and unintended consequences: State racial disparities imprisonment. Washington, DC: The Sentencing Project; Bridges, G. & Crutchfield, R.D. (1982). Law, social standing and racial disparities in imprisonment, *Social Forces*, 66(3): 699-724.

13. Data from Massachusetts in this report should be interpreted with caution. The system of incarceration in Massachusetts is somewhat unique in that this state uses county-level houses of corrections to hold some inmates who have been convicted of felonies and sentenced up to 2.5 years. The population of prisoners in houses of corrections is approximately 5,400, but the racial composition of those incarcerated at these institutions is not publicly reported. For this reason, estimates in this report do not include inmates in houses of corrections. As a result, the rates of incarceration by race and ethnicity are underestimated. For more on the composition of Massachusetts prison system, see: Massachusetts Department of Corrections (2014). Weekly Count Sheets.

14. Blumstein, A. (1993). Racial disproportionality of U.S. prison populations revisited. University of Colorado Law Review 64(3); 743-760; Bridges, G. and Crutchfield, R. D. (1988). Law, social standing and racial disparities in imprisonment. *Social Forces* 66(3): 699-724; Mauer, M. (1997) Intended and unintended consequences: State racial disparities in imprisonment. Washington, DC: The Sentencing Project; Sorenson, J., Hope, R., & Stemen, D. (2003). Racial disproportionality in state prison admissions: Can regional variation be explained by differential arrest rates? Journal of Criminal Justice 31: 73-84; Mauer, M. & King, R. (2007). Uneven justice: State rates of incarceration by race and ethnicity. Washington, DC: The Sentencing Project; Tonry, M. (1994). Racial Disproportions in US Prisons. *British Journal of Criminology* 34 (1): 97-115; Tonry, M (2011). Punishing race. Oxford: Oxford University Press.

15. Garland, B., Spohn, C., and Wodahl, E. (2008). Racial disproportionality in the American prison population: Using the Blumstein method to address the critical race and justice issues of the 21st Century. *Justice Policy Journal* 5(2): 1-42.

16. Blumstein, A. (1993). Racial disproportionality of U.S. prison populations revisited. *University of Colorado Law Review* 64(3): 743-760.

17. Baumer, E. (2010). Reassessing and redirecting research on race and sentencing. Draft manuscript prepared for Symposium on the Past and Future of Empirical Sentencing for Research, School of Criminal Justice, University at Albany; Tonry, M. (2011). *Punishing race: An American dilemma continues.* New York: Oxford University Press.

18. Blumstein, A. (1982). On the racial disproportionality of United States' prison populations. *The Journal of Criminal Law and Criminology* 73(2): 1259-1281.; Garland, B., Spohn, C., and Wodahl, E. (2008). Racial disproportionality in the American prison population: Using the Blumstein method to address the critical race and justice issues of the 21st Century. *Justice Policy Journal* 5(2): 1-42.

19. Crawford, C., Chiricos, T., & Kleck, G. (1998). Race, racial threat, and sentencing of habitual offenders. *Criminology* 36: 481-511; Spohn, C., & Cederblom, J. (1991). Race

and disparities in sentencing: A test of the liberation hypothesis. *Justice Quarterly,* 8, 305-327.

20. Langan, P (1985). Racism on trial: New evidence to explain the racial composition of prisons in the United States. Journal of Criminal Law and Criminology 76: 666-683; Garland, B., Spohn, C., and Wodahl, E. (2008). Racial disproportionality in the American prison population: Using the Blumstein method to address the critical race and justice issues of the 21st Century. *Justice Policy Journal* 5(2): 1-42.

21. Baumer, E. (2010). Reassessing and redirecting research on race and sentencing. Draft manuscript prepared for Symposium on the Past and Future of Empirical Sentencing for Research, School of Criminal Justice, University at Albany; Garland, B.E., Spohn, C. and Wodahl, E.J. (2008). Racial disproportionality in the American prison population: Using the Blumstein method to address the critical race and justice issue of the 21st Century. *Justice Policy Journal* 5(2): 1-42.; and Bridges, G. & Crutchfield, R.D. (1988). Law, social standing and racial disparities in imprisonment. Social Forces 66(3): 699-724; Tonry, M. and Melewski, M. (2008). "The malign effects of drug and crime control policy on Black Americans." In Tonry, M. (ed.) *Crime and Justice: A review of research* (pp 1-44). Chicago: University of Chicago Press.

22. For a review of a number of studies that have applied Blumstein's formula to identify the amount of disproportionality that can be attributed to crime, as measured by arrest, see: Garland, B.E., Spohn, C. and Wodahl, E.J. (2008). Racial Disproportionality in the American Prison Population: Using the Blumstein Method to Address the Critical Race and Justice Issue of the 21st Century. *Justice Policy Journal* 5(2): 1-42.

23. Mauer, M. & King, R. (2007). Uneven justice: State rates of incarceration by race and ethnicity. Washington, DC: The Sentencing Project; Bridges, G. & Crutchfield, R. D. (1988). Law, social standing, and racial disparities in imprisonment. *Social Forces* 66(3): 699-724.

24. Armstrong, G. & Rodriguez, N. (2005). Effects of individual and contextual characteristics on preadjudication detention of juvenile delinquents. *Justice Quarterly* 22(4): 521-539.

25. Baumer, E. (2010). Reassessing and redirecting research on race and sentencing. Draft manuscript prepared for Symposium on the Past and Future of Empirical Sentencing for Research, School of Criminal Justice, University at Albany.

26. Kutateladze, B., Andirilo, N., Johnson, B.D., & Spohn, C.C. (2014). Cumulative disadvantage: Examining racial and ethnic disparity in prosecution and sentencing. *Criminology* 52 (3): 514-551.

27. Frost, N., & Clear, T. (2013). *The punishment imperative: The rise and failure of mass incarceration in America.* New York: New York University Press.

28. Zimring, F. (2010). The scale of imprisonment in the United States: Twentieth Century patterns and Twenty-First Century prospects. *The Journal of Criminal Law and Criminology* 100(3): 1225-1241.

29. Rothwell, J. (2015). Drug offenders in American prisons: The critical difference between stock and flow. Washington, DC: Brookings Institution.

30. Mauer, M. (2009). The changing racial dynamics of the war on drugs. Washington, DC: The Sentencing Project.

31. Fagan, J. (2010). Second supplemental report, *Floyd v The City of New York*, 2013 U.S. District. LEXIS 68790 (S.D.N.Y. 2013). (08 Civ. 01034).

32. Schnake, T., Jones, M., & Brooker, C. (2010). The history of bail and pretrial release. Washington, DC: Pretrial Justice Institute.

33. Spohn, C. (2000). Thirty years of sentencing reform: The quest for a racially neutral sentencing process. In Policies, Processes, and Decisions of the Criminal Justice System, Volume 3, 427-501: page 481.

34. Crawford, C., Chiricos, T., & Kleck, G. (1998). Race, racial threat, and sentencing of habitual offenders. *Criminology* 36(3): 481-511.

35. Crawford, C., Chiricos, T., & Kleck, G. (1998). Race, racial threat, and sentencing of habitual offenders. Criminology 36(3): 481-511; Caravelis, C., Chricos, T., & Bales, W. (2013). Race, ethnicity, threat, and the designation of career offenders. *Justice Quarterly* 30(5): 869-894.

> *"Even though Muslims do not commit acts of terrorism in the United States at higher levels than other communities, Muslims are disproportionately targeted by government counterterrorism policies."*

Mandatory Minimum Sentences Are Handed Out Disproportionally to Ethnic Minorities

Sameer Ahmed

In the following excerpted viewpoint, Sameer Ahmed argues that the United States' aggressive War on Terror policies since 9/11 have led to significant prison sentences for many young American Muslims, even when their charged criminal conduct cannot be tied to any act of violence in the United States or abroad. A primary reason provided for their severe punishment is that these individuals are uniquely dangerous, cannot be deterred or rehabilitated, and must be incapacitated to protect society from their ideologically violent goals. In the 1980s and 1990s, similar accusations were raised in the War on Drugs against young African Americans, who were described as remorseless "super-predators," and received lengthy sentences in an effort to reduce drug and gang violence across the United States. Sameer Ahmed is a graduate of Yale Law School.

"Is History Repeating Itself? Sentencing Young American Muslims in the War on Terror," by Sameer Ahmed, *The Yale Law Journal*, March 2017. Reprinted by permission.

As you read, consider the following questions:

1. What is the primary reason why individuals convicted of terrorism-related conduct have received extraordinarily long criminal sentences?
2. What are the negative effects of lengthy incarceration on African American and Muslim American communities?
3. What have advocates and academics argued about changes in terrorism sentencing laws that are necessary to establish more effective and just policies?

Since 9/11, the US government has undertaken an aggressive War on Terror to target violent extremist groups like Al Qaeda and ISIS that are based in Muslim-majority countries. In recent years, a handful of violent shootings and bombings by self-identified Muslims in Boston, San Bernardino, and Orlando—in addition to more deadly attacks in Europe, Africa, South Asia, and the Middle East—have exacerbated fears of terrorism and the need to combat it. For the most part, the United States has adopted a zero-tolerance, preventative counterterrorism strategy of arresting anyone who may support foreign terrorist groups and incapacitating them with lengthy terms of incarceration. Federal law enforcement has a variety of tools at its disposal to implement this policy, including "material support for terrorism" statutes to prosecute offenders and sentencing guidelines to put them away for decades in prison. These tactics have been used even when the offenders' conduct cannot be tied to any act of violence in the United States or abroad. A primary justification given for these extraordinarily punitive measures is that those affiliated with terrorist activity—primarily young Muslim men—are uniquely dangerous: because they cannot be deterred or rehabilitated, they must instead be incapacitated to protect society from their ideologically violent goals.

Twenty to thirty years ago, similar accusations were levied against another group of individuals—young African American men—in the War on Drugs. Concerned about the rise of drug and gang violence in the 1980s and 1990s, government officials argued that remorseless inner-city "super-predators" must be incapacitated to stem the tide of death and destruction across the United States.[1] To address the problem, the government instituted a series of harsh penalties to significantly increase the criminal sentences for a wide range of drug-related conduct. However, the majority of individuals sentenced were not hardened violent criminals, but rather nonviolent low-level drug offenders.[2] Many now recognize that these War on Drugs policies have caused significant and disproportionate harm to African American communities, where one-third of African American men are expected to be incarcerated during their lifetime.[3] In recent years, changes in Supreme Court precedent, the United States Sentencing Guidelines, and charging policies have led to a reduction in the length of drug-related sentences, and policymakers have focused on alternative means of addressing drug crimes and rehabilitating offenders.

Similar to the War on Drugs, many of the individuals that have been sentenced in the War on Terror are not hardened remorseless terrorists. In fact, a number are young, disaffected American Muslims with little to no criminal history, whose anger over the killings of Muslims throughout the Middle East and the discrimination against Muslims in the United States has made them susceptible to the views of terrorist groups like ISIS.[4] Furthermore, just like the War on Drugs, the government's sentencing policies—in particular the Sentencing Guidelines' Terrorism Enhancement—fail to take into account the differences between a violent terrorist who has killed dozens and an American Muslim teenager who tweets support for ISIS online. Despite these similarities, this Feature contends that the lessons learned from counterproductive War on Drugs sentencing laws have not yet been translated to the War on Terror. Instead, terrorism sentencing policies have caused harm to Muslim communities similar to that of African American communities in the War on Drugs. This is despite the fact that Muslims convicted of terrorism offenses make up only a few hundred of the millions of Muslims living in the United

States.[5] And, like the War on Drugs, the War on Terror policies have failed to serve the purposes of criminal sentencing or to contribute to an effective counterterrorism policy.

[…]

Criminal Sentencing in the Wars on Terror and Drugs

Soon after 9/11, the US government launched the War on Terror to destroy Al Qaeda and other like-minded terrorist groups that threatened the United States and its allies.[6] As part of the War on Terror, the government adopted a strategy of proactively preventing terrorist attacks before they take place and incapacitating any individual who supports terrorist organizations. Attorney General John Ashcroft instructed the Department of Justice to "prevent first, prosecute second."[7] To achieve this goal, the government expanded a series of laws and policies to allow law enforcement officials to arrest individuals well before they can commit or support violent acts and sentence them to lengthy terms of incarceration.[8] These changes included broadening the Sentencing Guidelines Terrorism Enhancement and federal terrorism statutes.[9] As George Brown writes, "If prevention is at the heart of counter-terrorism, harsh sentences seem appropriate here as well."[10] The government does not want to "wait until there are victims of terrorist attacks to fully enforce the nation's criminal laws against terrorism."[11]

The Sentencing Guidelines Terrorism Enhancement

The primary reason why individuals convicted of terrorism-related conduct have received extraordinarily long criminal sentences is due to section 3A1.4 of the United States Sentencing Guidelines, also known as the "Terrorism Enhancement."[12] The Terrorism Enhancement significantly increases the sentencing range (known as the "Guidelines range") that federal judges use when deciding the appropriate term of incarceration.

The Terrorism Enhancement is just one of many adjustments contained in the Guidelines created by the United States Sentencing Commission.[13] The Guidelines establish various sentencing ranges based on a chart cross-referencing forty-three "offense levels" with six "criminal history" categories.[14] For example, someone convicted of a serious crime with an offense level of forty-two and a lengthy criminal history (Category VI) would receive a Guidelines range of 360 months to life, while someone convicted of a lesser crime with an offense level of twelve and very little criminal history (Category I) would receive a Guidelines range of ten to sixteen months.[15] The Guidelines also contain many adjustments based on the characteristics of the offense, the offender, or the victim.[16] The adjustments can increase or decrease the offense level and/or the criminal history category. The Terrorism Enhancement is one such adjustment.

While federal judges were originally required to sentence defendants within the calculated Guidelines range, in 2005 the Supreme Court in *United States v. Booker* struck down the mandatory Guidelines regime as unconstitutional.[17] Although the Guidelines are now only advisory, they continue to be the starting point to calculate the sentence for every federal offense, and courts, for the most part, attempt to sentence individuals within the range. For example, in 2015, 76.6% of defendants received a sentence either within the Guidelines range or below the range when the proposed sentence was sponsored by the prosecution.[18] Moreover, if a court elects to impose a sentence outside the range, it must demonstrate why it is reasonable to do so.[19] Therefore, the Guidelines, including the Terrorism Enhancement, still play an important role in determining the sentences of individuals convicted of terrorism offenses.

The Terrorism Enhancement was created pursuant to the Violent Crime Control and Law Enforcement Act of 1994, where Congress directed the Sentencing Commission "to provide an appropriate enhancement for any felony, whether committed within or outside the United States, that involves or is intended to promote international terrorism, unless such involvement or intent is itself an element of the crime."[20]Although the Enhancement initially applied only to international terrorism, the Antiterrorism and Effective Death Penalty Act of 1996 expanded the Terrorism Enhancement to apply to domestic terrorism as well.[21]After 9/11, the USA PATRIOT Act further expanded the Enhancement, making it applicable to a broad category of terrorism-related offenses, including: (1) crimes involving terrorism, but not falling within the statutory definition of "federal crime of terrorism"; (2) obstructing an investigation of a federal crime of terrorism; (3) harboring or concealing a terrorist; and (4) intending to influence the government's conduct by intimidation or coercion, retaliate against government conduct, or influence a civilian population by intimidation or coercion.[22] In addition to the commission of the actual crime, the Terrorism Enhancement also applies to inchoate offenses.[23] Therefore, while the Guidelines usually permit an offense level reduction for uncompleted crimes under section 2X1.1(b),[24] for terrorism offenses, defendants who conspire or attempt to commit a crime are treated exactly the same as those who actually commit the crime.

Although the Terrorism Enhancement has been expanded significantly to apply to a broad range of conduct, its effect on an individual's sentence has remained the same since its enactment. A defendant's offense level is increased by twelve levels, but cannot be lower than thirty-two.[25] His criminal history category is also increased to Category VI, the highest level.[26] The minimum Guidelines range under the Terrorism Enhancement is 210 to 262 months (17.5 to 21.8 years).[27] Of all the adjustments in the Guidelines, the Terrorism Enhancement is the most severe.[28] As an example, the Enhancement can lead to a sentence from thirty years to life for a crime that would otherwise result in a sentence of around five years.

[...]

Justifying Lengthy Sentences in the Wars on Terror and Drugs

Although neither the terrorism nor the drug sentencing laws discussed above explicitly targeted one specific religious, ethnic, or racial group, both the Wars on Terror and Drugs have disproportionately affected particular segments of the American public: Muslims and African Americans, respectively. With the War on Terror, even though Muslims do not commit acts of terrorism in the United States at higher levels than other communities,[63] Muslims are disproportionately targeted by government counterterrorism policies.[64] The reason is obvious. The primary focus of the War on Terror has not been to eliminate all forms of terrorism, but rather to combat violent attacks from Al Qaeda—the perpetrators of the 9/11 attacks—and like-minded groups such as ISIS.[65] Similarly, with the War on Drugs, even though they were no more likely than whites to use or sell illegal drugs,[66] African Americans were far more likely to be arrested for drug crimes, and received much stiffer sentences.[67] This too was based on government objectives not to focus on all drug crimes, but rather primarily those that were tied to gang violence in predominantly African American communities.[68]

Interestingly, when justifying the application of these stringent sentencing policies to young American Muslims and African Americans, policymakers and commentators have used notably similar reasons: these dangerous individuals are uniquely incapable of being rehabilitated and deterred in the short-term and must be incapacitated with lengthy terms of incarceration. And, in both cases, these justifications are unsupported. Instead, the punishment given to many American Muslims and African Americans has been much "greater than necessary" to achieve the purposes of federal sentencing.[69]

Justification for Terrorism Sentencing

As explained above, unlike in other contexts, terrorism sentencing fails to sufficiently address how much harm the defendant has caused, and instead the Terrorism Enhancement creates lengthy sentences for a broad range of conduct.[70] Legislators and courts have justified adopting these long sentences based on their view that terrorism as an offense, and terrorists as individuals, are uniquely situated among all crimes and criminals, which supports fundamentally altering the sentencing process.

When Congress requested that the Sentencing Commission enact the Terrorism Enhancement in 1994, the Commission had initially expressed reservations because the proposed adjustment would not take into account the fact that "defendants who share a common terrorist objective may vary greatly in terms of the threat to persons and national security that they realistically pose."[71] In response, the Chair of the Attorney General's Subcommittee on Sentencing Guidelines disregarded the Commission's nuanced view of terrorism offenses and instead urged the Commission to enact the Enhancement "in order to combat this serious threat to public safety."[72] For this reason, as Second Circuit Judge Walker explains, the Terrorism Enhancement "reflects Congress' [sic] and the Commission's policy judgment that an act of terrorism represents a particularly grave threat because of the dangerousness of the crime and the difficulty of deterring and rehabilitating the criminal, and thus that terrorists and their supporters should be incapacitated for a longer period of time" than other criminals.[73]Courts have thus justified applying the Terrorism Enhancement by stating that "terrorists[,] [even those] with no prior criminal behavior[,] are unique among criminals in the likelihood of recidivism, the difficulty of rehabilitation, and the need for incapacitation."[74] As Wadie Said notes, this belief "that terrorism is different, maybe even exceptional" is premised on "a type of visceral outrage at all conduct linked to terrorists that can taint the individualized and careful process that is supposed to go into a criminal sentencing" and "justifies a departure from the normal standards."

[…]

The Negative Effects of Lengthy Incarceration on African American and American Muslim Communities

The faulty premise underlying sentencing policies in the Wars on Drugs and Terror has not only led to significant prison sentences for many young African Americans and American Muslims. It has also caused harm to African American and American Muslim communities more broadly in similar ways. These negative effects include (1) increasing discrimination by reinforcing stereotypes of African Americans and Muslims as inherently dangerous, (2) furthering distrust of law enforcement among African Americans and Muslims, which undermines government objectives by making these communities less likely to cooperate in criminal investigations, and (3) failing to effectively rehabilitate drug and terrorism offenders and reintegrate them into society.

The harsh sentencing laws in the War on Drugs have had profound, negative consequences for African American communities throughout the United States. For example, the prison level for African Americans convicted of drug-related offenses in 2000 was twenty-six times that in 1983.[192] In some communities, three-fourths of African American men have served prison time, and more African Americans are in prison or under correctional supervision than were enslaved in 1850.[193] This mass incarceration has led to the discrimination and stigmatization of young African American men, significant distrust of law enforcement in African American communities, and the failure to effectively rehabilitate offenders during and after their sentences.

First, the myth of the "super-predator" and high incarceration rates have caused discrimination against African American men from a public who view them as exceptionally dangerous.[194] Not only have African Americans been disproportionately targeted by the police, they have also faced discrimination in a variety of areas, including employment, housing, and access to public services.[195] This mistreatment is due in part to stereotypes of young African Americans as drug offenders and criminals based on the media hysteria created in the aftermath of the crack-cocaine epidemic and inner-city gang violence that led to the creation of harsh criminal penalties in the War on Drugs.

[...]

Differences Between Communities Affected by the War on Drugs and Terror

Before comparing the harms faced by African American communities in the War on Drugs and those faced by American Muslims in the War on Terror, I must first acknowledge important demographic differences between the two groups. The population of Muslims in the United States is much smaller than the population of African Americans, and the percentage of Muslims convicted of terrorism-related crimes is also much smaller than the percentage of African Americans convicted of drug-related crimes. While the Muslim American population has been estimated to be at most six to seven million,[201] forty-two million identify as African American.[202] Furthermore, as explained above, drug-sentencing policies have had a widespread impact on African Americans.[203] The same cannot be said for terrorism sentencing policies' effect on Muslims, as only a few hundred have been charged with terrorism offenses, and the vast majority reject the violent extremist ideology of foreign terrorist organizations.[204]

For the most part, these differences do not affect the arguments made in this Feature. They have no effect on how young African American and Muslim men have been viewed as uniquely dangerous in the Wars on Drugs and Terror, respectively, leading to harsh sentencing policies in both contexts. They do, however, demonstrate why the consequences of the War on Drugs in the United States has affected a much larger segment of the American population than those of the War on Terror. This helps explain why African American communities have been more successful in advocating for community policing reforms than their Muslim counterparts have been in changing federal counterterrorism policies.[205] Since terrorism offenders make up a much smaller percentage of American Muslims, one might also expect that they would not be stereotyped in the same way as African Americans. However, because Muslims are also a much smaller percentage of the US population, many Americans do not personally know any Muslims, which, as demonstrated below, leads to high levels of discrimination toward Muslims and association of Muslims with violence.

[…]

Conclusion

Similar to the War on Drugs, the War on Terror has led to the imposition of lengthy criminal sentences for young nonviolent offenders. These policies disproportionately target a particular minority community, resulting in sentences that are contrary to the purposes delineated by Congress in 18 U.S.C. § 3553(a) and that undermine effective government policies to combat harm in the United States. In the War on Drugs, recent changes in judicial precedent, the Sentencing Guidelines, and charging policies have led to a reduction in the length of sentences, and policymakers have focused on alternative means of addressing drug-related crimes and rehabilitating offenders. For the most part, similar reforms have not been made in the War on Terror.

In recent years, advocates and academics have argued that changes in terrorism sentencing laws are necessary to establish more effective and just policies. Said recommends "that some combination of Congress, the US Sentencing Commission, and the federal courts establish standards to help courts better decide when a heightened punishment might be warranted, free from unsupported assumptions about the nature of terrorism or a particular defendant."[286] Skinner calls for "a new sentencing framework" based on "reasonableness (proportionality and necessity), and mitigating (and aggravating) circumstances."[287] The new framework would "provide courts with legal tools to distinguish between gradations of terrorist conduct" and "consider[] a defendant's 'substantial steps' toward the terrorism offense and the motives for his conduct."[288] Human Rights Watch asks the Sentencing Commission to "[c]onduct a study assessing whether the current system of sentence enhancements for terrorism is furthering appropriate criminal justice goals and is well-tailored to best meet those goals" and narrow the Terrorism Enhancement "to apply only to federal crimes of terrorism, as defined in 18 U.S.C. § 2332b(g)."[289] Dratel argues that prosecutors and judges should use 18 U.S.C. § 2339B(c), which authorizes the use of civil injunctive authority in material support cases, to order nonviolent terrorism offenders to participate in rehabilitation programs in lieu of criminal incarceration.[290]

These potential reforms would be important steps in addressing many of the problems analyzed in this Feature. However, it is unlikely that any will be implemented by government officials, at least in the short-term. Americans today view terrorism much differently than "ordinary" violent crimes or drug crimes.[291] The "super-predator"—a remorseless young African American man bent on creating havoc through gang and drug violence—has been replaced by the "terrorist"—a remorseless young Muslim man bent on killing as many Americans as possible. Until the discourse shifts to a more nuanced and realistic framing of the range of individuals convicted of terrorism crimes—as well as the actual threat faced by the United States—changes to the current sentencing framework are unlikely. Given that Donald Trump, who has advocated banning all Muslims from entering the United States, was elected President, the country appears to be moving in the opposite direction.

[...]

Endnotes

1. John J. Dilulio Jr., The Coming of the Super-Predators, WKLY. STANDARD (Nov. 27, 1995), http://www.weeklystandard.com/the-coming-of-the-super-predators/article/8160 [http:// perma.cc/NX9W-BYHZ].

2. See infra Section I.B.

3. Thomas P. Bonczar, Special Report: Prevalence of Imprisonment in the U.S. Population, 1974- 2001, BUREAU JUST. STAT. 1 (Aug. 2003), http://www.bjs.gov/content/pub/pdf/piusp01.pdf [http://perma.cc/N7UA-3JDR]; Jonathan Rothwell, How the War on Drugs Damages Black Social Mobility, BROOKINGS INSTITUTION (Sept. 30, 2014), http://www.brookings.edu/blog/social-mobility-memos/2014/09/30/how-the-war-on-drugs-damages-black-social-mobility [http://perma.cc/YHP8-J6U4].

4. See infra Section II.A.2.

5. By the Numbers: U.S. Prosecutions of Jihadist Terror Crimes, 2001-2013, CTR. ON NAT'L SECURITY FORDHAM L. [hereinafter By the Numbers], http://static1.squarespace.com/static/55dc76f7e4b013c872183fea/t/56b88ef1356fb0ff251aa15a/1454935794120/JihadistFactSheet2001-13.pdf [http://perma.cc/SB8Z-S72B]; Muslim Americans: Middle Class and Mostly Mainstream, PEW RES. CTR. 11 (May 22, 2007), http://www.pewresearch.org/files/2007/05/muslim-americans.pdf [http://perma.cc/9PH2-TX9D].

6. President George W. Bush, Address to a Joint Session of Congress and the American People, WHITE HOUSE (Sept. 20, 2001), http://georgewbush-whitehouse.archives.gov/news/releases/2001/09/20010920-8.html [http://perma.cc/D6WP-K8DQ].

7. Homeland Defense: Hearing Before the S. Comm. on the Judiciary, 107th Cong. 9 (2001) (statement of John Ashcroft, Att'y Gen. of the United States).

8. George D. Brown, Punishing Terrorists: Congress, the Sentencing Commission, the Guidelines, and the Courts, 23 CORNELL J. L. & PUB. POL'Y 517, 547-48 (2014).

9. See, e.g., Uniting and Strengthening America by Providing Appropriate Tools Required To Intercept and Obstruct Terrorism Act of 2001 (USA PATRIOT Act), Pub. L. No. 107-56, 115 Stat. 272.

10. Brown, supra note 8, at 547.

11. United States v. Abu Ali, 528 F.3d 210, 264 (4th Cir. 2008) (internal quotation marks omitted); see also Joshua L. Dratel, The Literal Third Way in Approaching "Material Support for Terrorism": Whatever Happened to 18 U.S.C. § 2339B(C) and the Civil Injunctive Option?, 57 WAYNE L. REV. 11, 80 (2011) ("The government's preemptive strategy has also resulted in the expansion of inchoate crimes such as attempt and conspiracy, as making arrests earlier along the time continuum further distances the defendant's conduct from a completed substantive crime, or even an agreement to commit a specific offense.").

12. U.S. SENTENCING GUIDELINES MANUAL § 3A1.4 (U.S. SENTENCING COMM'N 2015).

13. Sentencing Reform Act of 1984, Pub. L. No. 98-473, 98 Stat. 1987, 1989-90 (codified as amended at 18 U.S.C. § 3553 (2012)).

14. U.S. SENTENCING GUIDELINES MANUAL 403-04 tbl. (U.S. SENTENCING COMM'N 2015).

15. Id.

16. Id. at 343-74.

17. United States v. Booker, 543 U.S. 220, 226-27, 267 (2005).

18. National Comparison of Sentence Imposed and Position Relative to the Guideline Range, Fiscal Year 2015, U.S. SENT'G COMMISSION tbl.N (2015), http://www.ussc.gov/sites/default/files/pdf/research-and-publications/annual-reports-and-sourcebooks/2015/TableN.pdf [http://perma.cc/7T9V-V6GX].

19. *United States v. Stewart*, 590 F.3d 93, 134-35 (2d Cir. 2009).

20. Violent Crime Control and Law Enforcement Act of 1994, Pub. L. No. 103-322, § 120004, 108 Stat. 1796, 2022 (1994).

21. Antiterrorism and Effective Death Penalty Act of 1996, Pub. L. No. 104-132, § 730, 110 Stat. 1214, 1303.

22. Uniting and Strengthening America by Providing Appropriate Tools Required To Intercept and Obstruct Terrorism Act of 2001 (USA PATRIOT Act), Pub. L. No. 107-56, 115 Stat. 272; U.S. SENTENCING GUIDELINES MANUAL app. C, amend. 637 (U.S. SENTENCING COMM'N 2002); id. § 3A1.4 cmt. n.4.

23. See, e.g., *United States v. Wright*, 747 F.3d 399, 407 (6th Cir. 2014).

24. U.S. SENTENCING GUIDELINES MANUAL § 2X1.1(b) (U.S. SENTENCING COMM'N 2015).

25. Id. § 3A1.4(a).

26. Id. § 3A1.4(b).

27. Id. 403-04 tbl.

28. See Illusion of Justice: Human Rights Abuses in US Terrorism Prosecutions, COLUM. L. SCH. HUM. RTS. INST. & HUM. RTS. WATCH 124 (July 21, 2014) [hereinafter Illusion of Justice], http://www.hrw.org/report/2014/07/21/illusion-justice/human-rights-abuses-us-terrorism-prosecutions [http://perma.cc/56DJ-YLRM].

63. CHARLES KURZMAN, MUSLIM-AMERICAN TERRORISM IN 2014 2-3 (2015); Non-Muslims Carried Out More than 90% of All Terrorist Attacks on U.S. Soil, WASHINGTON'S BLOG (May 1, 2013), http://www.washingtonsblog.com/2013/05/muslims-only-carried-out-2-5-percent-of-terrorist-attacks-on-u-s-soil-between-1970-and-2012.html [http://perma.cc/RQN4-LSLA] (noting that only 2.5% of all terrorist attacks on U.S. soil between 1970 and 2012were carried out by Muslims).

64. Aziz Z. Huq et al., Why Does the Public Cooperate with Law Enforcement? The Influence of the Purposes and Targets of Policing, 17 PSYCHOL. PUB. POL'Y & L. 419, 423 (2011) ("Post-9/11 changes to policing strategies have been primarily targeted towards Muslim, South Asian and Arab Americans." (citations omitted)); id. ("Terrorism-related criminal investigations by the Federal Bureau of Investigation[] and local law enforcement focus disproportionately on mosques and Muslim civic organizations." (citations omitted)).

65. See National Strategy for Counterterrorism, WHITE HOUSE 3 (2011), http://www.whitehouse.gov/sites/default/files/counterterrorism_strategy.pdf [http://perma.cc/6BA4-L343] ("The preeminent security threat to the United States continues to be from al-Qa'ida and its affiliates and adherents." (emphasis and footnote omitted)); see also id. at 10-17 (describing the areas of focus of U.S. counterterrorism strategy).

66. See Rothwell, supra note 3.

67. Punishment and Prejudice: Racial Disparities in the War on Drugs, HUM. RTS. WATCH (May 2000) [hereinafter Punishment and Prejudice], http://www.hrw.org/legacy/reports/2000/usa/Rcedrg00-04.htm [http://perma.cc/JB4C-EUQP].

68. See MICHAEL TONRY, MALIGN NEGLECT—RACE, CRIME AND PUNISHMENT IN AMERICA (1995); Moriearty & Carson, supra note 52, at 290; Punishment and Prejudice, supra note 67.

69. Contra 18 U.S.C. § 3553(a) (2012) ("The court shall impose a sentence . . . not greater than necessary . . . .").

70. Said, supra note 50, at 527 (noting that "modern terrorism prosecution now relies largely on material support charges unconnected to any violence and inchoate criminal activity not likely to result in actual violence").

71. U.S. SENTENCING COMM'N, ANALYSIS OF THE VIOLENT CRIME CONTROL AND LAW ENFORCEMENT ACT OF 1994: PART II, at 13 (1994).

72. Hearing Before the U.S. Sentencing Comm'n Concerning Proposed Sentencing Guideline Amendments 20 (Mar. 14, 1995) (statement of Jay P. McClosky, U.S. Attorney, District of Maine & Chairman, Subcommittee on Sentencing Guidelines, Att'y Gen.'s Advisory Comm. of U.S. Attorneys, & Robert S. Litt, Deputy Assistant Att'y Gen., Criminal Division); see also *United States v. Stewart*, 590 F.3d 93, 172 (2d Cir. 2009) (Walker, J., concurring in part and dissent-ing in part) ("Congress expressly mandated that the Sentencing Commission provide for a terrorism enhancement to ensure that crimes of terrorism were met with a punishment that reflects their extraordinary seriousness.").

73. Stewart, 590 F.3d at 172-73 (Walker, J., concurring in part and dissenting in part) (emphasis and quotations omitted).

74. *United States v. Jayyousi*, 657 F.3d 1085, 1117 (11th Cir. 2011); *United States v. Meskini*, 319F.3d 88, 92 (2d Cir. 2003); see also Said, supra note 50, at 481 ("At the heart of [terrorism sentencing case law] lies a message that terrorism is especially heinous, and those convicted of terrorist crimes are particularly dangerous to the point of being irredeemably incapable of deterrence.").

192. JEREMY TRAVIS, BUT THEY ALL COME BACK: FACING THE CHALLENGES OF PRISONER REENTRY 28 (2005).

193. Michelle Alexander, The New Jim Crow, 9 OHIO ST.J. CRIM. L. 7, 9 (2011).

194. Huq & Muller, supra note 60, at 4.

195. See, e.g., Jillian Berman, The Job Market Discriminates Against Black College Grads, HUFFINGTON POST (May 20, 2014), http://www.huffingtonpost.com/2014/05/20/black-college-graduates_n_5358983.html [http://perma.cc/H7P7-A8XU]; Shaila Dewan, Discrimination in Housing Against Nonwhites Persists Quietly, U.S. Study Finds, *New York Times* (June 11, 2013), http://www.nytimes.com/2013/06/12/business/economy/discrimination-in-housing-against-nonwhites-persists-quietly-us-study-finds.html [http://perma.cc/8DGV-HEW7]; Corrado Giulietti et al., Racial Discrimination in Local Public Services: A Field Experiment in the US (Inst. for the Study of Labor, Discussion Paper No. 9290, 2015), http://ftp.iza.org/dp9290.pdf [http://perma.cc/7DKY-EEGC].

201. Muslim Americans: Middle Class and Mostly Mainstream, PEW RES. CTR. 11 (May 22, 2007), http://www.pewresearch.org/files/2007/05/muslim-americans.pdf [http://perma.cc/9PH2-TX9D].

202. Sonya Rastogi et al., The Black Population: 2010, U.S. CENSUS BUREAU 3 (Sept. 2011), http://www.census.gov/prod/cen2010/briefs/c2010br-06.pdf [http://perma.cc/5822-S223].

203. See supra Section III.A.

204. CHARLES KURZMAN, THE MISSING MARTYRS: WHY THERE ARE SO FEW MUSLIM TERRORISTS 11 (2011); Tyler et al., supra note 197, at 366 ("Recent studies suggest that [American Muslims] generally express strong allegiance to America and very little support for terrorism or terrorists."); By the Numbers, supra note 5.

285. See Aziz, supra note 151, at 210-11.

286. Said, supra note 50, at 481-82.

287. Skinner, supra note 32, at 345.

288. Id. at 349, 357.

289. Illusion of Justice, supra note 28, at 185.

290. Dratel, supra note 11, at 93 (noting that, pursuant to their discretionary equitable authority, "courts can be innovative and affirmative in imposing customized conditions such as . . . counseling and other programming (including vocational if appropriate), religious instruction, some form of supervision and reporting, restricted internet access, associational and travel limitations, financial monitoring, and even home detention and/or electronic monitoring" (footnote omitted)).

291. See Buchhandler-Raphael, supra note 213, at 848 ("[S]ince the September 11 attacks, fear and anxiety have dominated the public's perception of actors who are labeled 'terrorists,' and therefore using the 'terrorism' rhetoric critically influences public perceptions of crime and punishment."); id. (noting that with the War on Terror "powerful emotions, particularly hatred and fear, often prevail over rational legal doctrines, resulting in significant deviations in criminal law and procedure" (internal quotation marks omitted)); Huq et al., supra note 64, at 423 (noting that "people may respond differently to counterterrorism policing than to crime-control because they view terrorism as imposing a graver risk of harm to individuals than the more diffuse consequences of ordinary crime" and "may have different normative assessments of crime and terrorism").

> "*The Fair Sentencing Act sought to correct penalties associated with certain types of drug convictions, however, some critics believe that the Fair Sentencing Act did not go far enough.*"

The Fair Sentencing Act Did Not Go As Far As It Could Have

HG.org Legal Resources

In the following viewpoint, HG.org Legal Resources argues that a number of important laws have been passed in the twenty-first century that have changed the landscape of how defendants charged with drug crimes are prosecuted and sentenced. The move has been to decrease the sentences given to individuals in possession of small amounts of drugs and to reform existing laws so that minority individuals are not given harsher sentences that are targeted to affect their communities more than others. The Fair Sentencing Act sought to correct penalties associated with certain types of drug convictions, however, some critics believe that the Fair Sentencing Act did not go far enough. HG.org is an online law and government information resource.

"New Law Changes Mandatory Minimums, but More Must Be Done," HG.org Legal Resources. Reprinted by permission.

As you read, consider the following questions:

1. The Fair Sentencing Act reduced the possible sentence by making a conviction for crack cocaine how many times greater than the crime for powder cocaine?
2. What is the United States Sentencing Commission responsible for?
3. Why are mandatory minimum sentences often criticized, according to the viewpoint?

A number of important laws have been passed in the 21st century that have changed the landscape of how defendants charged with drug crimes are prosecuted and sentenced. The move has been to decrease the sentences given to individuals in possession of small amounts of drugs and to reform existing laws so that minority individuals are not given harsher sentences that are targeted to affect their communities more than others.

Fair Sentencing Act

On August 3, 2010 President Barack Obama made the Fair Sentencing Act. The law sought to correct penalties associated with certain types of drug convictions after years of sentiments that they were overly harsh and unjust. Historically, the punishments associated with crack cocaine in comparison to powder cocaine were much stricter. Traditionally, it took 100 times more powder cocaine as crack cocaine to get the same sentence. This was perceived over time as a discriminatory practice targeted at inner-city defendants who were typically of minority populations.

The Fair Sentencing Act reduced the possible sentence by making a conviction for crack cocaine only 18 times greater than the crime for powder cocaine. Additionally, it increased the amount of crack cocaine that a defendant would have to be in possession of to trigger the five-year and ten-year mandatory minimum sentences. It also eliminated the mandatory minimum for simple possession of crack cocaine.

The law was the first of its kind to be passed that repealed a mandatory minimum sentence for the first time since President Richard Nixon's administration. The law is expected to provide fairer sentences for about 2,000 offenders charged each year.

However, some critics believe that the Fair Sentencing Act did not go far enough. The original incarnation of the bill would have eliminated the disparity between crack and powder cocaine and the 18:1 change was a compromise. Additionally, the law did not provide retroactive application, so many inmates are still serving time under the harsh sentences that existed prior to the passage of the act.

United States Sentencing Commission Reform

Another influential change is reform to sentencing guidelines by the United States Sentencing Commission. This commission is responsible for establishing the guidelines that courts consult when doling out punishments. Some federal mandatory minimum drug sentences are from 5 to 40 years. Recent reforms have reduced sentences related to crack cocaine and other drug offenses. A report by the United States Sentencing Commission has found that the number of federal prison inmates convicted under mandatory minimum sentenced were 14 percent less in 2016 compared to 2010.

Legalization of Marijuana

Another significant change that has occurred during the 21st century is the decriminalization of marijuana. Some states have altogether made marijuana legal including for recreational purposes. Others have permitted its use for specific medical purposes, allowing individuals to carry a card or other certificate that indicates the medical use. Still others have demoted the crime of possessing a small amount of marijuana from a misdemeanor to a petty offense that only requires the payment of a small fine.

Cash Bail

Minority defendants make up a disproportionate number of indigent defendants. Therefore, when cash bail is ordered, they may be unable to pay it. Some states have moved to eliminate cash bail completely for low-level drug crimes. Under these systems, defendants are released on their ow recognizance or have community members vouch for them instead of expecting large sums of money upfront before any guilt has been proven.

Elimination of Mandatory Minimum Sentences

Some states like South Carolina and Rhode Island have eliminated mandatory minimum sentences for drug charges. Mandatory minimum sentences are often criticized for taking the discretion of sentencing away from judges and giving the prosecutors the power. Additionally, opponents to mandatory minimum sentencing guidelines argue that prosecutors use steep mandatory minimum sentencing guidelines to coerce defendants to plead guilty—even if they are not.

Drug Diversion

Another move that many communities have made is to offer drug diversion programs, drug counseling, drug courts and other alternatives to traditional sentencing plans. Many critics cite the expense related to keeping so many prisoners behind bars due to excessive sentences related to drug crimes.

Continued Reform

The Fair Sentencing Act was a bipartisan effort that was approved by a voice vote. No roll call was necessary. Continued bipartisan support may help continue the trend to reduce excessive penalties for defendants and to find more effective ways of preventing the commission of drug activity. There continues to be a need for additional reform.

> "As policy views have shifted over time, Congress and many others have continued to examine the role and scope of these mandatory minimum penalties in the federal criminal system."

The Justice Safety Valve Act of 2013 Allows Judges to Avoid Applying Mandatory Minimum Sentences

US Sentencing Commission

In the following excerpted viewpoint, the United States Sentencing Commission looks at the impact of mandatory minimum sentences on federal sentencing. It highlights recent developments regarding the charging of offenses carrying a mandatory minimum penalty and provides updated sentencing data regarding the use and impact of mandatory minimum penalties. It explains how offenders can obtain sentencing relief through the statutory "safety valve" by providing "substantial assistance" to authorities in the investigation. As directed by Congress, the Commission incorporated this statutory mechanism for relief from mandatory minimum penalties into the guidelines. The United States Sentencing Commission is a bipartisan independent agency that collects, analyzes, and distributes a broad array of information on federal sentencing practices.

Source: US Sentencing Commission. June 2017. www.ussc.gov.

As you read, consider the following questions:

1. What did the commission uniformly conclude in its 2011 Mandatory Minimum report?
2. Under the current system, a sentencing court can impose a sentence below an otherwise applicable statutory mandatory minimum penalty under what conditions?
3. The safety valve only applies if which five criteria are met?

This publication assesses the impact of mandatory minimum penalties on federal sentencing. It continues the United States Sentencing Commission's work in this area by highlighting recent developments regarding the charging of offenses carrying a mandatory minimum penalty, and providing updated sentencing data regarding the use and impact of mandatory minimum penalties. This publication builds on the Commission's previous reports and publications—particularly, its 2011 Report to the Congress: Mandatory Minimum Penalties in the Federal Criminal Justice System—and is intended to contribute to the continued examination of federal mandatory minimum penalties. It is the first in a series, with future publications focusing on mandatory minimum penalties for specific offense types.

Federal statutory mandatory minimum penalties have existed since the early days of the nation,[1] and they have continually evolved in the centuries since. As policy views have shifted over time, Congress[2] and many others[3] have continued to examine the role and scope of these mandatory minimum penalties in the federal criminal system.[4] For more than thirty years, the United States Sentencing Commission ("the Commission")[5] has played a central role in this process, working with the legislative, executive, and judicial branches of government and other interested parties to ensure that sentencing policy promotes the goals of the Sentencing Reform Act of 1984 ("SRA").[6]

Consistent with its statutory role,[7] the Commission has continued to inform the ongoing discussion regarding sentencing policy by gathering, analyzing, and disseminating sentencing data, including analyses regarding the use, scope and impact that mandatory minimum penalties have on sentencing in the federal system. The Commission has submitted numerous reports to

Congress, released varying data publications, responded to Congressional data requests, and provided Congressional testimony regarding mandatory minimum penalties over the past 30 years.[8] The Commission submitted its first report to Congress about mandatory minimum penalties only a few years after the initial guidelines went into effect.[9] At that time, the Commission concluded that "the most ef cient and effective way for Congress to exercise its powers to direct sentencing policy is through the established process of the sentencing guidelines, permitting the sophistication of the guidelines structure to work, rather than through mandatory minimums."[10]

Most recently, the Commission issued its comprehensive 2011 Report to the Congress: Mandatory Minimum Penalties in the Federal Criminal Justice System (2011 Mandatory Minimum Report). That report, which was submitted pursuant to the statutory directive contained in section 4713 of the Matthew Shepard and James Byrd, Jr. Hate Crimes Prevention Act of 2009,[11] provided detailed historical analyses of the evolution of federal mandatory minimums,[12] scientific and medical literature on the topic, and extensive analysis of the Commission's own data, public comment, and expert testimony.[13]

While expressing a "spectrum of views" regarding mandatory minimum penalties in its 2011 Mandatory Minimum Report, the Commission uniformly concluded that "a strong and effective sentencing guidelines system best serves the purposes of the Sentencing Reform Act."[14] The Commission further concluded that where "Congress decides to exercise its power to direct sentencing policy by enacting mandatory minimum penalties, . . . such penalties should (1) not be excessively severe, (2) be narrowly tailored to apply only to those offenders who warrant such punishment, and (3) be applied consistently."[15]

Lastly, the Commission encouraged Congress to request prison impact analyses as early as possible in its legislative process whenever it considers enacting or amending criminal penalties to ensure that increasingly strained federal prison resources are focused on offenders who commit the most serious offenses.[16] Guided by these general principles, the Commission expressed its belief that the current system of mandatory minimum penalties could be improved, and made several specific recommendations regarding the four major offense types studied in the report.[17]

In conjunction with its concluding recommendations in the 2011 Mandatory Minimum Report, the Commission explained that it "stands ready to work with Congress on measures that can be taken to enhance the strength and effectiveness of the current guidelines system and address the problems with certain mandatory minimum penalties identi ed in this report."[18] To that end, the Commission has continued to provide timely and objective sentencing data, information, and analysis to assist the ef cient and effective exercise of congressional power to direct sentencing policy.

This publication continues the Commission's work in the area of federal mandatory minimums by highlighting recent developments, as well as providing updated sentencing data regarding the use and impact of mandatory minimum penalties. It analyzes the most recently available sentencing data to supplement the data presented in the 2011 Mandatory Minimum Report, providing a detailed empirical research study of the effect of mandatory minimum penalties under federal law, including an updated assessment of the impact of mandatory minimum sentencing provisions on the federal prison population.

Like the Commission's recent publications on recidivism of federal offenders,[19] this publication is designed to be the first in a series, with future publications focusing on mandatory minimum penalties for specific offense types.

[...]

Can Offenders Obtain Relief From Mandatory Minimum Penalties?

Not all offenders convicted of an offense carrying a mandatory minimum penalty are sentenced to the minimum term of imprisonment specified in the statute of conviction.[103] Under the current system,[104] a sentencing court can impose a sentence below an otherwise applicable statutory mandatory minimum penalty if: (1) the prosecution les a motion based on the defendant's "substantial assistance" to authorities in the investigation or prosecution of another person; or (2) in certain drug trafficking cases, the defendant qualifies for the statutory "safety valve" contained in 18 U.S.C. § 3553(f).

Substantial Assistance

Two related provisions allow a sentencing court to impose a term of imprisonment lower than a mandatory minimum penalty in cases where a defendant provides substantial assistance in the investigation or prosecution of another person: 18 U.S.C. § 3553(e) and Federal Rule of Criminal Procedure 35(b).

18 U.S.C. § 3553(e)

Section 3553(e), which was enacted as part of the Anti-Drug Abuse Act of 1986,[105] grants a court limited authority to impose a sentence below a mandatory minimum penalty at the time of sentencing. Specifically, the section provides that "[u]pon motion of the Government, the court shall have the authority to impose a sentence below a level established by statute as a minimum sentence so as to re ect a defendant's substantial assistance in the investigation or prosecution of another person who has committed an offense."[106] Section 3553(e) further requires such a sentence to "be imposed in accordance with the guidelines and policy statements issued by the Sentencing Commission pursuant to section 994 of title 28, United States Code."[107]

As directed by Congress, the Commission incorporated this statutory mechanism for relief from mandatory minimum penalties into the guidelines. USSG §5K1.1, consistent with the requirements of the Commission's organic statute,[108] authorizes a departure from the guideline range if the offender has provided substantial assistance to law enforcement. In contrast to section 3553(e), however, §5K1.1 does not explicitly authorize courts to impose a sentence below a mandatory minimum penalty but instead includes a reference to 18 U.S.C. § 3553(e).[109] As such, even if the government les a motion under §5K1.1, the sentencing court may not impose a sentence below a statutory mandatory minimum penalty unless the government also les a motion pursuant to 18 U.S.C. § 3553(e).[110]

Federal Rule of Criminal Procedure 35(b)

Relief under section 3553(e) is, in most respects, identical to the relief provided under Rule 35 of the Federal Rules of Criminal Procedure, as both require substantial assistance and both require a government motion. The most significant difference between the two types of motions is timing: Rule 35(b) motions are made after the original sentencing and so require a resentencing if granted, while section 3553(e) motions are made before sentencing and ruled on at the time of the original sentencing.[111]

Rule 35(b) permits a court, upon the government's motion, to impose a new, reduced sentence that considers post-sentencing substantial assistance. Rule 35(b)(1) provides that, "[u]pon the government's motion made within one year of sentencing, the court may reduce a sentence if the defendant, after sentencing, provided substantial assistance in investigating or prosecuting another person."[112] Pursuant to Rule 35(b)(2), motions may also be made later than one year after the original sentence if the "defendant's substantial assistance involved": (1) "information not known to the defendant until one year or more after sentencing," (2) information provided within one year that "did not become useful to the government until more than one year after sentencing," or (3) if the defendant could not have "reasonably . . . anticipated" that the information in question would be useful until more than a year after sentencing.[113] In evaluating whether the substantial assistance is, in fact, sufficient to warrant a reduction under Rule 35(b), "the court may consider the defendant's presentence assistance."[114]

Rule 35(b) expressly applies to sentences that would otherwise be subject to a mandatory minimum penalty, authorizing the sentencing court to "reduce the sentence to a level below the minimum sentence established by statute."[115]

Statutory "Safety Valve" Relief

The second relief provision, codified at 18 U.S.C. § 3553(f) (Limitation on Applicability of Mandatory Minimum Penalties in Certain Cases), is commonly referred to as the "safety valve."[116] Unlike a substantial assistance departure—which applies to all types of federal offenses carrying a mandatory minimum penalty—the safety valve statute only applies in cases in which a defendant faces a mandatory minimum penalty after being convicted of a drug trafficking offense listed in the statute.[117] In addition, the safety valve only applies if the following five criteria are met:

- the defendant does not have more than one criminal history point, as determined under the sentencing guidelines;
- the defendant did not use violence or credible threats of violence or possess a rearm or other dangerous weapon (or induce another participant to do so) in connection with the offense;
- the offense did not result in death or serious bodily injury to any person;
- the defendant was not an organizer, leader, manager, or supervisor of others in the offense, as determined by the sentencing guidelines and was not engaged in a continuing criminal enterprise, as defined in 21 U.S.C. § 848; and
- no later than the time of the sentencing hearing, the defendant has truthfully provided to the Government all information and evidence the defendant has concerning the offense or offenses that were part of the same course of conduct or of a common scheme or plan, but the fact that the defendant

has no relevant or useful or other information to provide or that the government is already aware of the information shall not preclude a determination by the court that the defendant has not complied with this requirement.

Where these criteria are met, section 3553(f) provides that judges shall impose a sentence without regard to the statutory mandatory minimum penalty for the covered offenses.

For defendants who qualify for relief from the mandatory minimum penalty pursuant to the statutory safety valve, the guideline at §5C1.2 directs the court to "impose a sentence in accordance with the applicable guidelines without regard to any statutory minimum sentence."[118] The drug trafficking guideline at USSG §2D1.1 also provides for a 2-level decrease if the defendant meets the safety valve subdivision criteria listed at USSG §5C1.2.[119] This decrease applies regardless of whether the defendant was convicted of an offense carrying a mandatory minimum penalty.[120]

[...]

Endnotes

1 As discussed in more detail in the Commission's 2011 report on mandatory minimum penalties, Congress created the first comprehensive series of federal offenses with the passage of the 1790 Crimes Act, which specified 23 federal crimes. See U.S. Sentencing comm'n, RepoRt to congReSS: mandatoRy minimUm penaltieS in the FedeRal cRiminal JUStice SyStem, at 7 (Oct. 2011), available at http://www.ussc.gov/research/congressional-reports/2011-report-congress-mandatory-minimum-penalties- federal-criminal-justice-system [hereinafter 2011 mandatoRy minimUm RepoRt] (citing Act of Apr. 30, 1790, Chap. IX, 1 Stat. 112). Seven of the offenses in the 1790 Crimes Act carried a mandatory death penalty: treason, murder, three offenses relating to piracy, forgery of a public security of the United States, and the rescue of a person convicted of a capital crime. See id.

2 See, e.g., Sentencing Reform Act of 2015, H.R. 3713 (first introduced Oct. 8, 2015); Sentencing Reform and Corrections Act of 2015, S. 2123 (first introduced Oct. 1, 2015). See also Smarter Sentencing Act of 2013, S. 1410. See also 156 CONG. REC. S1680–83 (daily ed. Mar. 17, 2010) and 156 CONG. REC. H6196–6204 (daily. ed. July 28, 2010) (for debate associated with passage of Fair Sentencing Act of 2010, Pub. L. No. 111–220, 124 Stat. 2372). See also 150 CONG. REC. H4808–11 (daily ed. June 23, 2004) and 150 CONG. REC. S7527 (daily ed. June 25, 2004) (for debate associated with passage of Identity Theft Penalty Enhancement Act, Pub. L. No. 108–275, 118 Stat. 831). See also 149 CONG. REC. S2573–90 (daily ed. Feb. 24, 2003), 149 CONG. REC. H2440–43 (daily ed. Mar. 27, 2003), 149 CONG. REC. H3059, 3066–76 (daily ed.

Apr. 10, 2003), 149 CONG. REC. H2950–68 (daily ed. Apr. 9, 2003), 149 CONG. REC. S5113–35, S5137–57 (daily ed. Apr. 10, 2003) (for debate associated with passage of Prosecutorial Remedies and Other Tools to end the Exploitation of Children Today Act of 2003, Pub. L. No. 108–21, 117 Stat. 650).

3 For a detailed historical discussion of varying policy views regarding the use of federal mandatory minimum penalties, see 2011 mandatoRy minimUm RepoRt, Ch. 5.

4 See 2011 Mandatory Minimum Report, Ch. 4(B). Overall, statutes carrying mandatory minimum penalties have increased in number, apply to more offense conduct, require longer terms, and are used more often than they were 20 years ago. These changes have occurred amid other systemic changes to the federal criminal justice system that also have had an impact on the size of the federal prison population. Those include expanded federalization of criminal law, increased size and changes in the composition of the federal criminal docket, high rates of imposition of sentences of imprisonment, and increasing average sentence lengths. The changes to mandatory minimum penalties and these co-occurring systemic changes have combined to increase the federal prison population significantly.

5 The United States Sentencing Commission ("Commission") is an independent agency in the judicial branch of government. Established by the Sentencing Reform Act of 1984, its principal purposes are (1) to establish sentencing policies and practices for the federal courts, including guidelines regarding the appropriate form and severity of punishment for offenders convicted of federal crimes; (2) to advise and assist Congress, the federal judiciary, and the executive branch in the development of effective and efficient crime policy; and (3) to collect, analyze, research, and distribute a broad array of information on federal crime and sentencing issues. See 28 U.S.C. §§ 995(a)(14), (15), (20).

6 Title II, Comprehensive Crime Control Act of 1984, Pub. L. No. 98–473 (1984).

7 See 28 U.S.C. §§ 995(a)(14)–(16), which collectively instruct the Commission to systematically collect and disseminate information regarding federal sentencing.

8 See, e.g., Statement of Judge Patti B. Saris, Chair, United States Sentencing Commission, For Hearing on "S. 212, Sentencing Reform and Corrections Act of 2015" Before the Committee on the Judiciary, United States Senate (Oct. 19, 2015), available at http:// www.ussc.gov/sites/default/ les/pdf/news/congressional-testimony-and-reports/ testimony/20151021_Saris_ Testimony.pdf; Statement of Judge Patti B. Saris, Chair, United States Sentencing Commission, For Hearing on "H.R. 3717, Sentencing Reform Act of 2015" Before the U.S. house of Representatives Judiciary Committee (Nov. 18, 2015), available at http:// www.ussc.gov/sites/default/ les/pdf/news/congressional-testimony-and-reports/submissions/20151117_HR3713.pdf.

9 See U.S. Sentencing comm'n, Special Report to congress: mandatory minimum penalties in the Federal criminal Justice System (as directed by Section 1703 oF public law 101–647) (Aug. 1991) [hereinafter 1991 mandatory minimum report].

10 See id. See also Hearing on Federal Mandatory Minimum Sentencing Before the Subcomm. on Crime and Criminal Justice of the H. Comm. on the Judiciary, 103rd Cong. (July 28, 1993) (statement of Hon. William W. Wilkins, Jr., Chairman, United States Sentencing Commission), reprinted in 6 Fed. Sentencing Rep. 67 (1993); Mandatory Minimum Sentencing Laws The Issues: Hearing Before the Subcomm. on Crime, Terrorism, and Homeland Sec. of the H. Comm. on the Judiciary, 110th Cong. 6 (2007) (statement of Hon. Ricardo H. Hinojosa, Chairman, United States Sentencing Commission); U.S. Sentencing comm'n, Report to congress regarding

Federal mandatory minimum Sentencing penalties (on record in Mandatory Minimums and Unintended Consequences, Hearing Before the Subcomm. on Crime, Terrorism, and Homeland Security of the H. Comm. on the Judiciary, 111th Cong. 124 (July 14, 2009)); Mandatory Minimum Penalties Hearing Before the U.S. Sentencing Commission (May 27, 2010).

11 Division E of the National Defense Authorization Act for Fiscal Year 2010, Pub. L. No. 111–84, 123 Stat. 2190, 2843 (enacted October 28, 2009). The Commission also submitted its 2011 mandatory minimum Report pursuant to its general authority under 28 U.S.C. §§ 994–995, and its specific authority under 28 U.S.C. § 995(a)(20) which provides that the Commission shall have authority to "make recommendations to Congress concerning modi cation or enactment of statutes relating to sentencing, penal, and correctional matters that the Commission nds to be necessary and advisable to carry out an effective, humane, and rational sentencing policy."

12 See 2011 mandatory minimum report, Chs. 2–5.

13 See id., Chs. 6–11.

14 See id., at Ch.12.

15 See id.

16 See id.

17 See id.

18 See id., at 369.

19 See, U.S. Sentencing comm'n, Recidivism among Federal Offenders: a Comprehensive Overview (Mar. 2016), available at http://www.ussc.gov/research/research-reports/recidivism-among-federal-offenders-comprehensive-overview; U.S. Sentencing comm'n, Recidivism among Federal Drug Trafficking Offenders (Feb. 2017), available at http://www.ussc.gov/ research/research-reports/recidivism-among-federal-drug-trafficking-offenders; U.S. Sentencing comm'n, Criminal History and Recidivism of Federal Offenders (Mar. 2017), available at http://www.ussc.gov/research/research-reports/criminal-history-and- recidivism-federal-offenders.

103 While this section focuses on mechanism for relief from a mandatory minimum penalty, some offenders are also sentenced to a term of imprisonment that is above the applicable mandatory minimum.

104 Various mechanisms have been in place permitting a court to impose a sentence lower than a mandatory minimum penalty in certain cases for more than a century. For example, even before statutory mechanisms were in place, district courts avoided imposing a term of imprisonment, even for offenses carrying a mandatory minimum penalty, by suspending the sentence or by placing the defendant under the supervision of a state probation o cer. For a detailed discussion of the historical development of such "relief" mechanisms, see 2011 mandatory minimum report, at 31–36.

105 See Pub. L. No. 99–570, 100 Stat. 3207 (1986).

106 18 U.S.C. § 3553(e). For additional discussion of section 3553(e) and relevant case law, development of such "relief" mechanisms, see 2011 mandatory minimum report, Appendix E(A)(2), (B)(3).

107 Id.

108 See 28 U.S.C. § 994(n) ("The Commission shall assure that the guidelines re ect the general appropriateness of imposing a lower sentence than would otherwise be imposed, including a sentence that is lower than that established by statute as a

minimum sentence, to take into account a defendant's substantial assistance in the investigation or prosecution of another person who has committed an offense.").

109 See USSG §5K1.1, comment. (n.1).

110 See *Melendez v. United States*, 518 U.S. 120 (1996).

111 For a detailed legal and statistical analysis of Rule 35, see U.S. Sentencing comm'n, the Use of Federal Rule of Criminal Procedure 35(b) (January 2016).

112 Fed. R. crim. p. 35(b)(2). Prior to the enactment of the Sentencing Reform Act, Rule 35(b) allowed the court to reduce a sentence for any reason within 120 days after the sentence was imposed or probation was revoked, and the court had authority to change a sentence from a term of incarceration to probation. See Fed. R. crim. p. 35(b) (1983). The Sentencing Reform Act amended Rule 35(b), however, making three significant changes. See Fed. R. crim. p. 35(b) (1986). First, the government was required to make a motion seeking a reduction, which deprived the court of authority to reduce a sentence on its own. Second, the time period was expanded from 120 days to one year. Third, the reduction was limited to reflect the defendant's "substantial assistance in the investigation or prosecution of another person who has committed an offense, in accordance with the guidelines and policy statements issued by the Sentencing Commission." Id. In addition, before the Act became effective, Congress added language to Rule 35(b) authorizing the court to reduce a sentence lower than the statutory minimum. See id. at 35(b)(2) ("When acting under Rule 35(b), the court may reduce the sentence to a level below the minimum sentence established by statute.").

113 Fed. R. crim. p. 35(b)(2). This language has changed substantially over time. From 1991 to 2002, the Rule permitted a motion after one year only if the defendant learned the information in question more than one year after sentencing. In 2002, the Rule was amended to incorporate the current, broader language. See Fed. R. crim. p. 35 advisory committee's notes, 2002 Amendments ("where the usefulness of the information is not reasonably apparent until a year or more after sentencing, no sound purpose is served by the current rule's removal of any incentive to provide that information to the government one year or more after the sentence (or if previously provided, for the government to seek to reward the defendant) when its substantiality become evident.").

114 Fed. R. crim. p. 35(b)(3). Before this language was added in 1998, some pre-sentencing assistance was not substantial enough to warrant a §5K1.1 motion; however, because of Rule 35's language, this assistance could also not then be considered on a Rule 35(b) motion. See, e.g., *United States v. Speed*, 53 F.3d 643, 645 (4th Cir. 1995); *United States v. Bureau*, 52 F.3d 584, 595 (6th Cir. 1995).

115 Fed. R. crim. p. 35(b)(4).

116 See Violent Crime Control and Law Enforcement Act of 1994, Pub. L. No. 103–322, § 80001, 108 Stat. 1796 (codified at 18 U.S.C. § 3553(f)). Enactment of the safety valve stemmed from the Commission's 1991 report on mandatory minimums and its subsequent work with Congress to enact new legislation that would address the impact of mandatory minimum penalties on low-level drug-trafficking offenders. See 2011 mandatory minimum report, at 34–36 (discussing the history of the statutory safety valve).

117 These offenses include an offense under section 401, 404, and 406 of the Controlled Substances Act (21 U.S.C. §§ 841 (possession with intent to distribute), 844 (possession), 846 (conspiracy)) or section 1010 or 1013 of the Controlled Substances Import and Export Act (21 U.S.C. §§ 961 (conspiracy), 963 (importation)). See 18 U.S.C. § 3553(f).

118 See USSG §5C1.2(a). As required by Congressional directive, the new offense level cannot be lower than 17 for offenders whose mandatory minimums were at least five years in length. See USSG §5C1.2(b).

119 See USSG §2D1.1(b)(17).

120 See USSG §2D1.1, comment. (n.21). This application note was added to the guidelines, effective November 1, 2002, that clarifies that the 2-level reduction does not depend on whether the defendant is convicted under a statute that carries a mandatory minimum term of imprisonment. See USSG App. C, amend. 640 (effective Nov. 1, 2002).

> *"Iowa imprisons a larger percentage of its African-American population than most states. Mandatory minimum sentences are driving that trend."*

Mandatory Minimum Sentences for Domestic Violence Will Hurt the African American Community

Leigh Goodmark

In the following viewpoint, Leigh Goodmark argues that, despite good intentions, the setting of mandatory minimum sentences for domestic violence in Iowa will actually do more harm than good. The author contends that the state of Iowa disproportionately imprisons African American men and that the new domestic abuse laws will only add to that. At a time when lawmakers are realizing that mandatory minimum sentences are not effective for other crimes, why would they think otherwise regarding domestic abuse crimes? The author suggests that those in power should instead work toward increasing employment opportunities. Leigh Goodmark is a professor of law at the University of Maryland, Baltimore. Her focus is gender violence.

As you read, consider the following questions:

1. What group did not support Iowa's bill, which set new mandatory minimum sentences for domestic abusers?
2. At what level are most domestic violence crimes prosecuted?
3. What does the author suggest might actually make a difference in minimizing domestic abuse?

O n March 8, the Iowa House of Representatives passed a bill setting new mandatory minimum sentences in domestic violence cases. Those convicted of domestic violence three times must serve 85 percent of their sentences prior to release, regardless of their conduct while imprisoned. The Iowa Senate voted unanimously to adopt the law on April 6.

Legislators lauded the bill's benefits for survivors of violence.

Those benefits, however, weren't as clear to the Iowa Coalition Against Domestic Violence, which opposed the provision. The coalition called the bill a well-intentioned but ultimately ineffective measure to prevent repeat domestic violence.

Social science research supports the coalition's position. Increasing jail time generally has a minimal effect on recidivism. Researchers have found limited to no relationship between jail time and repeat violence in domestic violence cases.

I'm a lawyer who represents survivors of intimate partner violence. Over the last 20 years, I have written extensively about the failures of the criminal system's response to domestic violence.

Increasing mandatory minimums in domestic violence cases is yet another misguided policy.

Minimums Harm African-American Men

Here's what the new Iowa measure is likely to do: increase the number of African American men imprisoned in the state.

As the *Des Moines Register* has reported, approximately 35 percent of the inmates serving mandatory minimum sentences in Iowa prisons are African-American.

African-Americans make up only 3.4 percent of the Iowa's population. Iowa imprisons a larger percentage of its African-American population than most states. Mandatory minimum sentences are driving that trend.

Iowa recognizes the problematic consequences of mandatory minimum sentences. For three years, Iowa's Public Safety Advisory Board has recommended that legislators move away from mandatory minimums. This year, Iowa legislators approved a bill giving judges greater sentencing discretion in some cases. Yet in the same session, the legislature voted to create new mandatory minimum sentences for domestic violence.

This inconsistency isn't specific to Iowa. The same thing is happening on the national level.

Last year's Sentencing Reform and Corrections Act was intended to address the US problem with mass incarceration. The bill decreases mandatory minimum sentences for a number of federal crimes.

Most domestic violence crimes are prosecuted at the state level. The Sentencing Reform and Corrections Bill looked only at the small subset of domestic violence crimes that fall under federal jurisdiction. These are crimes that occur when someone travels from one state to another to commit an act of domestic violence. Forcing or tricking someone into traveling between states and harming that person also falls within the definition.

Sentences for interstate domestic violence already range from five years to life, depending upon the severity of the crime. The act would increase those penalties significantly. As in Iowa, support for the change came from lawmakers, not advocates. In fact, the National Task Force to End Sexual and Domestic Violence Against Women came out against a similar provision in 2013. The task force noted in particular the harmful impact of mandatory minimum sentences on communities of color.

In a Nutshell

Mandatory minimum sentencing laws require binding prison terms of a particular length for people convicted of certain federal and state crimes. These inflexible, "one-size-fits-all" sentencing laws may seem like a quick-fix solution for crime, but they undermine justice by preventing judges from fitting the punishment to the individual and the circumstances of their offenses. Mandatory sentencing laws cause federal and state prison populations to soar, leading to overcrowding, exorbitant costs to taxpayers, and diversion of funds from law enforcement.

Most mandatory minimum sentences apply to drug offenses, but Congress has enacted them for other crimes, including certain gun, pornography, and economic offenses. Many states also have mandatory sentencing laws, but some have reformed them.

"What Are Mandatory Minimums?" Families Against Mandatory Minimums.

Domestic Violence Exceptionalism

At a time when most policymakers are moving away from mandatory minimum sentences, why should domestic violence be treated differently?

Like some advocates, I believe it shouldn't. But the response to domestic violence has been marked by a sense that it is somehow different from other crimes. This notion is known as "domestic violence exceptionalism."

Exceptionalism has been used to justify a number of criminal policies specific to domestic violence, including mandatory arrest, mandatory prosecution and lax application of the rules of evidence. And exceptionalism seems to be driving the efforts to increase sentences for domestic violence at a time when policymakers generally seem to understand that what the United States needs is less criminalization, not more.

Criminalization has been the primary policy response to domestic violence in the United States for the last 40 years. It is not working.

Since 1984, the US has committed hundreds of millions of dollars to the law enforcement response to domestic violence. The crime rate in the United States has been falling for some time. Rates of domestic violence have dropped in recent years. But despite the increased funding for and emphasis on policing and prosecuting domestic violence, rates of domestic violence have fallen less than the decline in the overall crime rate.

Ending domestic violence requires that people who use violence change their behavior. Mandatory minimum sentences don't create that kind of behavior change.

We should instead put resources into policies that might actually make a difference. One example: domestic violence is correlated with male under- and unemployment. Increasing employment opportunities for men who abuse could decrease rates of violence and create economic benefits for underresourced communities.

President Obama's Council of Economic Advisers recently declared that higher salaries would reduce crime more than increased incarceration. States considering new mandatory minimums for domestic violence would get more for their money by increasing the minimum wage instead.

Periodical and Internet Sources Bibliography

The following articles have been selected to supplement the diverse views presented in this chapter.

Charles L. Betsey, "Income and Wealth Transfer Effects of Discrimination in Sentencing," The Review of Black Political Economy/Winter-Spring 2005.

Audrey Bomse, Sharlyn Grace, and the Mass Incarceration Committee of the NLG, "Moving Beyond Brock Turner: Focusing on Mass Incarceration, *Guild Notes*, Winter 2016, Vol. 42 Issue 4.

J. Zamgba Browne, "NAACP Leadership Blasts Mandatory Minimum Sentencing," *New York Amsterdam News*, 08/03/2000, Vol. 91, Issue 31.

Alan Dahl, "Eric Holder's Recent Curtailment of Mandatory Minimum Sentencing, Its Implications, and Prospects for Effective Reform," *BYU Journal of Public Law.* 2014, Vol. 29 Issue 1, pp. 271–297. 27p.

Federal Bureau of Prisons, Statistics: Inmate Ethnicity, May 30, 2015. https://www.bop.gov/about/statistics/statistics_inmate_ethnicity. jsp.

Stephanie Findlay, "Trouble in the Big House," *Maclean's*, January 24, 2011, Vol. 124, Issue 2.

John Fulmer, "U.S. Sentencing Commission Survey: Many Judges Think Mandatory Minimums Lengthy," *Daily Record* (Rochester, NY). June 16, 2010.

Brandon Gee, "Sentencing Panel Eyes 'Safety Valve' Proposal," *Massachusetts Lawyers Weekly,* October 22, 2015.

Kevin Johnson, "Prison Proposal Gains Backing," *USA Today*, August 13, 2013.

Wendy Kaminer, "Mandatory Sentences and Myths of Equal Justice," The Atlantic Monthly Group, December 22, 2010. https://www. theatlantic.com/national/archive/2010/12/mandatory-sentences- and-myths-of-equal-justice/68399.

Joseph Shapiro, "As Court Fees Rise, The Poor Are Paying The Price," NPR, May 19, 2014. http://www.npr.org/2014/05/19/312158516/ increasing-court-fees-punish-the-poor.

OPPOSING
VIEWPOINTS®
SERIES

CHAPTER 4

How Do Mandatory Minimum Sentences Impact the Crime Rate?

Chapter Preface

The point of mandatory minimum sentencing is crime reduction. These laws have drastically affected the operation of the various aspects of the justice system. But these laws have not caused the effect of full incarceration that their drafters might have wanted. A greater proportion of offenders eligible for mandatory sentences do not receive them; but for the most part, these offenders are probably punished more severely than if a mandatory sentence had not hung over their guilty pleas. A much smaller proportion of offenders are actually sentenced under these laws. And for them, there is no doubt that the punishments are more severe than was typical before these laws were implemented.

To supporters, the narrower-than-expected application of these laws or their adverse impact on the judicial system doesn't matter as long as the laws serve the greater good of preventing serious crime. But it is difficult to prove a deterrent effect.

What is known about the deterrent effect of the legislation is that it works best on people who have something to lose if they are punished. The rational choice is to not engage in criminal behavior, unless one is so poor or emotionally disturbed as to have nothing to lose by breaking the law. Rational criminals are more deterred by the likelihood that they will be caught at all than by the severity of possible punishment. Thinking about possible punishments deters few of them from the much more powerful daily rhythms of a way of life.

Compared to the general deterrent effect of mandatory sentencing, incarceration is probably more powerful. Felons in prison cannot commit crimes at the same rate as before. Models based on data from actual offenders show that incarceration from three-strike laws does reduce felony crime. Reductions vary depending on which crimes are governed as "strikes" and how often they will be applied.

> *"The judge's duty is not to promote public safety; it is to ensure that parties before the court receive justice."*

Mandatory Minimum Sentences Discourage People from Committing Crimes

Andrew C. McCarthy

In the following viewpoint, Andrew C. McCarthy argues that it is a bad idea to roll back mandatory minimum sentences. "These are terms of imprisonment, often harsh ones that must be imposed for serious crimes," he says. "Mandatory minimums tie the hands of judges, mandating that they take hard criminals off the streets rather than slap them on the wrists," he adds. "It is the latest Beltway fashion to demand that mandatory minimums be rolled back, if not repealed, on the theory that incarceration causes rather than drastically reduces crime." The author concludes with a final reminder that criminals should not be rewarded with lighter sentences. Andrew C. McCarthy is a senior fellow at the National Review Institute and a contributing editor of National Review.

As you read, consider the following questions:

1. Before the Reagan era, what were federal penal laws like?
2. If the judge's duty is not to promote public safety, what is it their responsibility to do?
3. A "reform" that reduces mandatory minimums will benefit only which class of people?

I know you lied in your testimony, but I understand why you believed you had to do it." If there was an audible sound in the courtroom after these words left the lips of the sentencing judge, it was my jaw caroming off the floor. I was a young prosecutor and it was the mid Eighties, before federal sentencing reforms substituted the public's sensibilities for the judges' in the matter of serious crime.

The defendant had been convicted of selling cocaine, an offense he compounded by perjuring himself in testimony so absurd that even my novice cross-examiner's skills were enough to expose it. The judge was a notoriously defendant-friendly sentencer, but even jurists of that bent of mind do not like having their intelligence insulted: When a serious felony was complemented by blatant lying under oath, a serious jail sentence was in order.

But not this time. To my dismay, the judge shrugged his shoulders and did what lots of judges did in those days, and what Washington's bipartisan political class seems to want them to start doing again: He walked the defendant out the door.

Thirty years have not dimmed the memory of what was then a commonplace. Young Americans for whom the Reagan administration is ancient history, New Yorkers who grew up in the post-Giuliani City—they have no memory of what it was like from the Sixties into the early Eighties.

For them, the revolution in crime-fighting that so dramatically improved the quality of American life is not revolutionary. It is simply . . . life. There is nothing hard-won about it. It is not informed by the dark days when rampant crime was fueled by a criminal-rights campaign premised on many of the same loopy ideas that undergird Washington's latest fetish, "sentencing reform."

The worst of those ideas is to roll back "mandatory minimum" sentences. These are terms of imprisonment, often harsh ones that must be imposed for serious crimes. Mandatory minimums tie the hands of judges, mandating that they take hard criminals off the streets rather than slap them on the wrists.

Before the Reagan era, federal penal laws prescribed potentially severe sentences for serious offenses—decades of jail time, up to life imprisonment. This reflected the judgment of the crime-plagued American people, as expressed by their representatives in Congress.

There was a big flaw in the system, though: The penal laws had no floors, no minimum amount of jail time that had to be imposed, significantly differentiating federal sentencing from state practice.

A defendant convicted of federal felonies—let's say heroin dealing or a violent extortion—might face a sentence of up to 50 years. Sounds draconian, but the reality was quite the opposite, because the judge was also free to impose the minimum sentence of no time whatsoever. What punishment to impose within that expansive statutory range from zero to 50 years was wholly the judge's call. In effect, this nearly boundless discretion transferred control over punishment for crime from the public to the courts.

Federal judges tend to be very good at the difficult job they are trained to do: apply law, which is frequently arcane and sometimes inconsistent, to factual situations, which have their own complexities. This skill, however, does not necessarily translate into expertise in making punitive judgments that are governed less by legal rules than gut feeling—gut feeling being what controls broad discretion.

This does not make Anthony Kennedy and his colleagues bad people. But it does illustrate that judges are not exactly the vox populi. They tend to be products of the schools in which they've excelled and the profession in which they've thrived.

Both the schools and the profession are considerably more left-wing than the public, on matters including those of crime and punishment. When the *New York Times* writes self-parodic headlines such as "Crime Rates Are Falling, but Prisons Keep on Filling," most of the public sensibly asks, "What do they mean but?" Many judges, to the contrary, think, "Yes, they have a point." And that was even before what will end up being close to 400 new judges were put on the bench by Barack Obama—a longtime criminal-rights advocate who once enthusiastically endorsed a book by former terrorist Bill Ayers that compares the US justice system to South African apartheid.

Even if many judges were not instinctively sympathetic to arguments against harsh sentencing, sympathy comes with the institutional territory. The judge's duty is not to promote public safety; it is to ensure that parties before the court receive justice. It is a bedrock conceit of those who toil in the justice system that the public perception of justice is just as vital as the objective reality of justice. Thus, the judge has great incentive to bend over backward to give convicted defendants every bounce of the due-process ball.

Add to that the human element: It is a lot easier to call for a harsh sentence from the peanut gallery than to be the judge who has to impose a sentence after a desperate plea for leniency has been made and while the defendant's mother, wife, and kids weep in the first row.

So whether the pressures were ideological, institutional, or rooted in human nature, judges were often weak sentencers. That weakness translated into the inadvertent promotion of crime by failing to disincentivize it and failing to sideline career criminals. Mandatory minimums were thus enacted by overwhelming congressional margins in order to divest judges of the discretion to impose little or no jail time for serious crimes and habitual criminals.

It is the latest Beltway fashion to demand that mandatory minimums be rolled back, if not repealed, on the theory that incarceration causes rather than drastically reduces crime. Or, since that claim doesn't pass the laugh test, on the theory that incarceration is racist—the great American conversation ender. Beyond the in terrorem effect of the racism smear, the latter rationale relies on the overrepresentation of minorities, particularly blacks and illegal aliens, in the prison population—and banks on your being too cowed to bring up the overrepresentation of minority communities in the crime-victim population.

Alas, a "reform" that reduces mandatory minimums will benefit only one class of people—serious felons who commit many more crimes than they are prosecuted for. And racism? Please. We have, to take one pertinent example, a harsh mandatory minimum sentence for predators who are convicted of a felony after having previously being convicted of three other serious crimes. Congress wasn't targeting race; it was targeting sociopaths.

Understand, I am not contending that the criminal-justice system is without flaws badly in need of correction. But the main problem is not severe sentencing. It is over-criminalization.

Too much formerly innocent private conduct has become prohibited, making criminals out of essentially law-abiding people. Law is supposed to be a reflection of society's values, not a tool by which society is coerced to transform its values. Moreover, when the statutes, rules, and regulations proliferate to the point that it becomes unreasonable to expect average people to know what is forbidden, we no longer have a nation of laws; we have a nation of men arbitrarily deciding which of the presumptively guilty get punished and which go unscathed.

If a problem is not accurately diagnosed, it will not be cured. There is a prescription for what ails us, but it is most certainly not a repeal of the severe sentences enacted to address serious crime. Nothing that rewards real criminals at the expense of the people they victimize should trade under the name of "reform."

> *"Despite substantial expenditures on longer prison terms for drug offenders, taxpayers have not realized a strong public safety return. Federal sentencing laws that were designed with serious traffickers in mind have resulted in lengthy imprisonment of offenders who played relatively minor roles."*

Federal Drug Sentencing Laws Bring High Cost and a Low Return

The Pew Charitable Trusts

In the following viewpoint, The Pew Charitable Trusts argues that changes in drug crime patterns and law enforcement practices have played a role in the explosion in prison populations. The authors claim that despite longer prison terms for drug offenders, Americans are not any safer because of it. In addition, federal sentencing laws that were designed to deter or punish serious traffickers have resulted in lengthy imprisonment of relatively minor players. These laws also have failed to reduce recidivism: one third of the drug offenders who leave federal prison and are placed on community supervision commit new crimes or violate the conditions of their release. The Pew Charitable Trusts is a non-governmental organization that strives to improve public policy.

As you read, consider the following questions:

1. What were some of the ways Congress increased drug penalties?
2. Just as enhanced criminal penalties have not reduced the availability or use of illegal drugs, what else does research show they are unlikely to do?
3. What is the federal government uniquely responsible for in the fight against the illegal drug trade?

More than 95,000 federal prisoners are serving time for drug-related offenses—up from fewer than 5,000 in 1980.[1] Changes in drug crime patterns and law enforcement practices played a role in this growth, but federal sentencing laws enacted during the 1980s and 1990s also have required more drug offenders to go to prison— and stay there much longer—than three decades ago.[2] These policies have contributed to ballooning costs: The federal prison system now consumes more than $6.7 billion a year, or roughly 1 in 4 dollars spent by the US Justice Department.[3]

Despite substantial expenditures on longer prison terms for drug offenders, taxpayers have not realized a strong public safety return. The self-reported use of illegal drugs has increased over the long term as drug prices have fallen and purity has risen.[4] Federal sentencing laws that were designed with serious traffickers in mind have resulted in lengthy imprisonment of offenders who played relatively minor roles.[5] These laws also have failed to reduce recidivism. Nearly a third of the drug offenders who leave federal prison and are placed on community supervision commit new crimes or violate the conditions of their release—a rate that has not changed substantially in decades.[6]

More Imprisonment, Higher Costs

Congress increased criminal penalties for drug offenders during the 1980s—and, to a lesser extent, in the 1990s—in response to mounting public concern about drug-related crime.[7] In a

1995 report that examined the history of federal drug laws, the US Sentencing Commission found that "drug abuse in general, and crack cocaine in particular, had become in public opinion and in members' minds a problem of overwhelming dimensions."[8] The nation's violent crime rate surged 41 percent from 1983 to 1991, when it peaked at 758 violent offenses per 100,000 residents.[9]

Congress increased drug penalties in several ways. Lawmakers enacted dozens of mandatory minimum sentencing laws that required drug offenders to serve longer periods of confinement. They also established compulsory sentence enhancements for certain drug offenders, including a doubling of penalties for repeat offenders and mandatory life imprisonment without the possibility of parole for those convicted of a third serious offense. These laws have applied broadly: As of 2010, more than 8 in 10 drug offenders in federal prisons were convicted of crimes that carried mandatory minimum sentences.[10]

Also during the 1980s, Congress created the Sentencing Commission, an appointed panel that established strict sentencing guidelines and generally increased penalties for drug offenses. The same law that established the commission, the Sentencing Reform Act of 1984, also eliminated parole and required all inmates to serve at least 85 percent of their sentences behind bars before becoming eligible for release.

Federal data show the systemwide effects of these policies:

- Probation has all but disappeared as a sanction for drug offenders. In 1980, federal courts sentenced 26 percent of convicted drug offenders to probation. By 2014, the proportion had fallen to 6 percent, with judges sending nearly all drug offenders to prison.[11]
- The length of drug sentences has increased sharply. As shown in Figure 1 above, from 1980 to 2011 (the latest year for which comparable statistics are available), the average prison sentence imposed on drug offenders increased 36 percent—from 54.6 to 74.2 months—even as it declined 3 percent for all other offenders.[12]

- The proportion of federal prisoners who are drug offenders has nearly doubled. The share of federal inmates serving time for drug offenses increased from 25 percent in 1980 to a high of 61 percent in 1994.[13] This proportion has declined steadily in recent years—in part because of rising prison admissions for other crimes—but drug offenders still represent 49 percent of all federal inmates.[14]
- Time served by drug offenders has surged. The average time that released drug offenders spent behind bars increased 153 percent between 1988 and 2012, from 23.2 to 58.6 months.[15] This increase dwarfs the 39 and 44 percent growth in time served by property and violent offenders, respectively, during the same period.[16]

The increased imprisonment of drug offenders has helped drive the explosive overall growth of the federal prison system, which held nearly 800 percent more inmates in 2013 than it did in 1980.[17] One study found that the increase in time served by drug offenders was the "single greatest contributor to growth in the federal prison population between 1998 and 2010."[18]

Growth in the prison population has driven a parallel surge in taxpayer spending. From 1980 to 2013, federal prison spending increased 595 percent, from $970 million to more than $6.7 billion in inflation-adjusted dollars.[19] Taxpayers spent almost as much on federal prisons in 2013 as they paid to fund the entire US Justice Department—including the Federal Bureau of Investigation, the Drug Enforcement Administration, and all US attorneys—in 1980, after adjusting for inflation.[20]

Increased Availability and Use of Illegal Drugs

Measurements of the availability and consumption of illegal drugs in the United States are imprecise. Users may be reluctant to share information about their illegal behavior, and national surveys may not capture responses from specific populations—such as homeless or incarcerated people—who may have high rates of drug use.

Drug markets also vary considerably from city to city and state to state, and among different drugs.

Despite these limitations, the best available data suggest that increased penalties for drug offenders—both at the federal and state levels—have not significantly changed long-term patterns of drug availability or use:

- Illegal drug prices have declined. The estimated street price of illegal drugs is a commonly cited measure of supply. Higher prices indicate scarcity while lower prices suggest wider availability. After adjusting for inflation, the estimated retail prices of cocaine, heroin, and methamphetamine all decreased from 1981 to 2012, even as the purity of the drugs increased.[21]
- Illegal drug use has increased. The share of Americans age 12 and older who said in a national survey that they had used an illicit drug during the previous month increased from 6.7 percent in 1990 to 9.2 percent—or nearly 24 million people—in 2012.[22] An increase in marijuana use helped drive this trend, more than offsetting a decline in cocaine use.

Just as enhanced criminal penalties have not reduced the availability or use of illegal drugs, research shows that they are unlikely to significantly disrupt the broader drug trade. One study estimated that the chance of being imprisoned for the sale of cocaine in the US is less than 1 in 15,000—a prospect so remote that it is unlikely to discourage many offenders.[23] The same applies for longer sentences. The National Research Council concluded in a 2014 report that mandatory minimum sentences for drug and other offenders "have few if any deterrent effects."[24] Even if street-level drug dealers are apprehended and incarcerated, such offenders are easily replaced, ensuring that drug trafficking can continue, researchers say.[25]

To be sure, many criminologists agree that the increased imprisonment of drug offenders—both at the federal and state levels—played a role in the ongoing nationwide decrease in crime that began in the early 1990s. But research credits the increased incarceration of drug offenders with only a 1 to 3 percent decline in the combined violent and property crime rate.[26] "It is unlikely that the dramatic increase in drug imprisonment was cost-effective," one study concluded in 2004.[27]

Penalties Do Not Match Roles

The federal government is responsible for combating illegal drug trafficking into the United States and across state lines. As a result, traffickers represent the vast majority of the drug offender population in federal prisons.[28] Federal sentencing laws have succeeded in incarcerating kingpins and other serious drug offenders for whom prison is the appropriate option. At the same time, however, they have resulted in the lengthy imprisonment of many offenders who played relatively minor roles in drug trafficking.

The Anti-Drug Abuse Act of 1986 demonstrates this trend. The law established a five-year mandatory minimum sentence for "serious" drug traffickers, defined as those convicted of crimes involving a minimum amount of illegal drugs, including 100 grams of heroin or 500 grams of cocaine. The law also created a 10-year mandatory minimum sentence for "major" traffickers—those convicted of crimes involving larger amounts, including 1 kilogram of heroin or 5 kilograms of cocaine.[29] Under the law, mandatory minimum sentences double from five to 10 years—and from 10 years to 20—for second offenses.

Although the law was intended to separate offenders into lower and higher degrees of culpability based on the amount of drugs involved in their crimes, these distinctions have not always captured individuals' true roles in drug distribution networks. "The quantity of drugs involved in an offense is not as closely related to the offender's function in the offense as perhaps Congress expected," the Sentencing Commission concluded in a special report to Congress in 2011.[30]

Historical data limitations make it difficult to assess whether the drug traffickers incarcerated in federal prisons today are more or less serious than those of three decades ago. But the Sentencing Commission's report underscores that federal resources have not been directed at the most serious drug traffickers.[31] According to the report, in 2009:

- Those sentenced for relatively minor roles represented the biggest share of federal drug offenders. More than a quarter of federal drug offenders—and two-thirds of federal marijuana offenders—were "couriers" or "mules," the lowest-level trafficking roles on a culpability scale developed by the commission.[32] The average sentences for couriers and mules—defined as those who transport illegal drugs either in a vehicle or on their person—were 39 and 29 months, respectively.

- Nearly a fifth of federal drug offenders were street dealers. Offenders defined as "street-level dealers"—those who distributed an ounce or less of illegal drugs directly to users—made up 17 percent of federal drug offenders and nearly half of federal crack cocaine offenders.[33] The average sentence for these individuals was 77 months.

- The highest-level traffickers represented a comparatively small share of federal drug offenders. Those defined as "high-level suppliers" or "importers"—the top function on the culpability scale—represented 11 percent of federal drug offenders. The average sentence for these offenders was 101 months.

- Sentence lengths did not always align with offenders' functions. Although lower-level functionaries generally received much shorter average sentences than higher-level offenders, there were notable exceptions: Midlevel "managers," for example, received an average sentence of 147 months, or nearly four years longer than the 101-month average sentence imposed on the highest-level traffickers.

It is important to note that federal law permits two exemptions to mandatory minimum sentences that frequently benefit many lower-level drug traffickers.[34] One allows sentence reductions for those who provide prosecutors with "substantial assistance" during the course of an investigation. The other, known as the "safety valve," applies to offenders who meet five specific criteria, including a limited criminal history and a nonleadership role in the drug trade.

Although these sentence reduction tools are intended to—and generally do—benefit low-level traffickers the most, there are exceptions. More than half of offenders deemed to be high-level suppliers or importers, for example, received relief from mandatory minimum penalties in 2009, compared with less than a third of those classified as street-level dealers—despite the much lower culpability level of the latter group.[35]

Post-Prison Outcomes Unchanged

Research has found little relationship between the length of prison terms and recidivism rates generally—a pattern that holds among drug offenders at the federal level.

Of the more than 20,000 federal drug offenders who concluded periods of post-release community supervision in 2012 (the latest year for which statistics are available), 29 percent either committed new crimes or violated the conditions of their release.[36] This proportion has changed little since the mid-1980s, when sentences and time served began increasing sharply.[37]

Conversely, targeted reductions in prison terms for certain federal drug offenders have not led to higher recidivism rates. In 2007, the Sentencing Commission retroactively reduced the sentences of thousands of crack cocaine offenders.[38] A follow-up study on the effects of this change found no evidence of increased recidivism among offenders who received sentence reductions compared with those who did not.[39] In 2010, Congress followed the Sentencing Commission's actions with a broader, statutory reduction in penalties for crack cocaine offenders.

Conclusion

The federal government has a uniquely important role to play in the fight against the illegal drug trade: It is responsible for preventing the trafficking of narcotics into the United States and across state lines. In response to rising public concern about high rates of drug-related crime in the 1980s and 1990s, Congress enacted sentencing laws that dramatically increased penalties for drug crimes, which in turn sharply expanded the number of such offenders in federal prison and drove costs upward. These laws—while playing a role in the nation's long and ongoing crime decline since the mid-1990s—have not provided taxpayers with a strong public safety return on their investment.

The availability and use of illegal drugs has increased even as tens of thousands of drug offenders have served lengthy terms in federal prisons. Recidivism rates for drug offenders have remained largely unchanged.

Meanwhile, federal sentencing laws that were designed to focus penalties on the most serious drug traffickers have resulted in long periods of imprisonment for many offenders who performed relatively minor roles in the drug trade.

In response to these discouraging trends, federal policymakers recently have made administrative and statutory revisions that have reduced criminal penalties for thousands of drug offenders while maintaining public safety and controlling costs to taxpayers.

Endnotes

1. For the current figure, see "Inmate Statistics—Offenses," Federal Bureau of Prisons, accessed June 29, 2015, http://www.bop.gov/about/statistics/statistics_inmate_offenses.jsp. For the 1980 figure, see University at Albany, Sourcebook of Criminal Justice Statistics 2003, Table 6.57, http://www.albany.edu/sourcebook/pdf/t657.pdf.

2. Nathan James, The Federal Prison Population Buildup: Overview, Policy Changes, Issues, and Options (Washington: Congressional Research Service, 2014), https://www.fas.org/sgp/crs/misc/R42937.pdf.

3. The Pew Charitable Trusts, "Federal Prison System Shows Dramatic Long-Term Growth" (February 2015), http://www.pewtrusts.org/~/media/Assets/2015/02/ Pew_Federal_Prison_Growth.pdf.

4. Office of National Drug Control Policy, National Drug Control Strategy: Data Supplement 2014, Tables 1 and 2, https://www.whitehouse.gov/sites/default/files/

ondcp/policy-and-research/ndcs_data_supplement_2014.pdf. Pew used the 1990-2012 period to capture all available yearly data.

5. U.S. Sentencing Commission, Report to the Congress: Mandatory Minimum Penalties in the Federal Criminal Justice System (October 2011), Chapter 8, http://www.ussc. gov/sites/default/files/pdf/news/congressional-testimony-and-reports/mandatory-minimum-penalties/20111031-rtc-pdf/Chapter_08.pdf.

6. Bureau of Justice Statistics, Federal Justice Statistics Statistical Tables Series 2005-2012, Compendium of Federal Justice Statistics Series 1984- 2004, http://www.bjs.gov/index. cfm?ty=tp&tid=65.

7. U.S. Sentencing Commission, Mandatory Minimum Penalties in the Federal Criminal Justice System, Chapter 2, http://www.ussc.gov/news/congressional-testimony-and-reports/mandatory-minimum-penalties/special-report-congress.

8. U.S. Sentencing Commission, Report on Cocaine and Federal Sentencing Policy, Chapter 6, http://www.ussc.gov/report-cocaine-and-federal- sentencing-policy-2.

9. Federal Bureau of Investigation, Uniform Crime Reporting data tool, http://www. ucrdatatool.gov.

10. U.S. Sentencing Commission, Report to the Congress: Mandatory Minimum Penalties in the Federal Criminal Justice System (October 2011), Chapter 8, 165, http://www. ussc.gov/sites/default/files/pdf/news/congressional-testimony-and-reports/mandatory-minimum-penalties/20111031-rtc-pdf/Chapter_08.pdf.

11. Administrative Office of the U.S. Courts, Judicial Business of the U.S. Courts Series, Table D-5, 1980-2014, http://www.uscourts.gov/statistics-reports/analysis-reports/ judicial-business-united-states-courts. The 1980 report is available in print only. In 1992, the end of the federal fiscal year changed from June 30 to Sept. 30.

12. Administrative Office of the U.S. Courts, Judicial Business of the U.S. Courts Series, Table D-5, 1980-2011. The 1980 report is available in print only. Figures calculated using weighted average sentences of drug offenders and nondrug offenders. Average does not include sentences of probation. In 2012, the Administrative Office of the U.S. Courts began calculating average sentence length using median months rather than mean months. As a result, comparable historical data are available only through 2011. In 1992, the end of the federal fiscal year changed from June 30 to Sept. 30.

13. University at Albany, Sourcebook of Criminal Justice Statistics 2003, Table 6.57, http:// www.albany.edu/sourcebook/pdf/t657.pdf.

14. "Inmate Statistics—Offenses," Federal Bureau of Prisons, accessed June 29, 2015, http://www.bop.gov/about/statistics/statistics_inmate_offenses.jsp.

15. For the 1988 figure, see Bureau of Justice Statistics, Federal Criminal Case Processing, 1982-93, Table 18, http://www.bjs.gov/content/pub/pdf/Fccp93.pdf; for the 2012 figure, see Bureau of Justice Statistics, Federal Justice Statistics 2012—Statistical Tables, Table 7.11, http://www.bjs.gov/content/pub/pdf/fjs12st.pdf. Pew used the 1988-2012 period to capture all available yearly data.

16. Ibid.

17. The Pew Charitable Trusts, "Federal Prison System Shows Dramatic Long-Term Growth."

18. Kamala Mallik-Kane, Barbara Parthasarathy, and William Adams, "Examining Growth in the Federal Prison Population, 1998 to 2010" (September 2012), Urban Institute,

http://www.urban.org/sites/default/files/alfresco/publication-pdfs/412720-Examining-Growth-in-the-Federal-Prison-Population—to—.PDF.

19. The Pew Charitable Trusts, "Federal Prison System Shows Dramatic Long-Term Growth."

20. Ibid.

21. Office of National Drug Control Policy, National Drug Control Strategy: Data Supplement 2014, Tables 66, 67, and 68, https://www.whitehouse.gov/sites/default/files/ondcp/policy-and-research/ndcs_data_supplement_2014.pdf.

22. Office of National Drug Control Policy, National Drug Control Strategy: Data Supplement 2014, Tables 1 and 2, https://www.whitehouse.gov/sites/default/files/ondcp/policy-and-research/ndcs_data_supplement_2014.pdf. Pew used the 1990-2012 period to capture all available yearly data.

23. David Boyum and Peter Reuter, An Analytic Assessment of U.S. Drug Policy, American Enterprise Institute for Public Policy Research (2005), 57, http://www.aei.org/wp-content/uploads/2014/07/-an-analytic-assessment-of-us-drug-policy_112041831996.pdf.

24. National Research Council, The Growth of Incarceration in the United States: Exploring Causes and Consequences (2014), 83, http://www.nap.edu/catalog/18613/the-growth-of-incarceration-in-the-united-states-exploring-causes.

25. Mark A.R. Kleiman, "Toward (More Nearly) Optimal Sentencing for Drug Offenders," Criminology & Public Policy 3, no. 3 (2004): 435–440, https://drive.google.com/file/d/0B6taQDF0rdAwYnJNTDU2bDVBNFU/edit.

26. Ilyana Kuziemko and Steven D. Levitt, "An Empirical Analysis of Imprisoning Drug Offenders," Journal of Public Economics 88 (2004): 2043–2066, https://www0.gsb.columbia.edu/faculty/ikuziemko/papers/kl_jpube.pdf.

27. Ibid.

28. U.S. Sentencing Commission, 2014 Sourcebook of Federal Sentencing Statistics, Table 12, http://www.ussc.gov/sites/default/files/pdf/research-and-publications/annual-reports-and-sourcebooks/2014/Table12.pdf.

29. U.S. Sentencing Commission, Report on Cocaine and Federal Sentencing Policy, Chapter 6, http://www.ussc.gov/report-cocaine-and-federal-sentencing-policy-2.

30. U.S. Sentencing Commission, Report to the Congress: Mandatory Minimum Penalties in the Federal Criminal Justice System (October 2011), Chapter 12, 350, http://www.ussc.gov/sites/default/files/pdf/news/congressional-testimony-and-reports/mandatory-minimum-penalties/20111031-rtc-pdf/Chapter_12.pdf.

31. Unless otherwise indicated, all data about offender roles are drawn from U.S. Sentencing Commission, Report to the Congress: Mandatory Minimum Penalties in the Federal Criminal Justice System (October 2011), Appendix D, Figure D-2, http://www.ussc.gov/sites/default/files/pdf/news/congressional-testimony-and-reports/mandatory-minimum-penalties/20111031-rtc-pdf/Appendix_D.pdf; and Figure 8-12, 173, http://www.ussc.gov/sites/default/files/pdf/news/congressional-testimony-and-reports/mandatory-minimum-penalties/20111031-rtc-pdf/Chapter_08.pdf.

32. For share of marijuana offenders considered mules or couriers, see U.S. Sentencing Commission, Report to the Congress: Mandatory Minimum Penalties in the Federal Criminal Justice System (October 2011), Appendix D, Figure D-34, http://www.ussc.

gov/sites/default/files/pdf/news/congressional-testimony-and-reports/mandatory-minimum-penalties/20111031-rtc-pdf/Appendix_D.pdf.

33. For share of crack cocaine offenders considered street-level dealers, see U.S. Sentencing Commission, Report to the Congress: Mandatory Minimum Penalties in the Federal Criminal Justice System (October 2011), Appendix D, Figure D-22, http://www.ussc.gov/sites/default/files/pdf/news/congressional-testimony-and-reports/mandatory-minimum-penalties/20111031-rtc-pdf/Appendix_D.pdf.

34. Charles Doyle, "Federal Mandatory Minimum Sentences: The Safety Valve and Substantial Assistance Exceptions" (Washington: Congressional Research Service, 2013), https://www.hsdl.org/?%20view&did=746019.

35. U.S. Sentencing Commission, Report to the Congress: Mandatory Minimum Penalties in the Federal Criminal Justice System (October 2011), Chapter 8, 170, http://www.ussc.gov/sites/default/files/pdf/news/congressional-testimony-and-reports/mandatory-minimum-penalties/20111031-rtc-pdf/Chapter_08.pdf.

36. Bureau of Justice Statistics, Federal Justice Statistics 2012—Statistical Tables, Table 7.5, http://www.bjs.gov/content/pub/pdf/fjs12st.pdf.

37. Bureau of Justice Statistics, Federal Justice Statistics/Compendium of Federal Justice Statistics Series, 1984-2012, http://www.bjs.gov/index.cfm?ty=pbtp&tid=65&iid=1. Data not available for 1987, 1991, 1992, and 2005.

38. U.S. Sentencing Commission, "U.S. Sentencing Commission Votes Unanimously to Apply Amendment Retroactively for Crack Cocaine Offenses" (Dec. 11, 2007), http://www.ussc.gov/news/press-releases-and-news-advisories/december-11-2007.

39. Kim Steven Hunt and Andrew Peterson, "Recidivism Among Offenders Receiving Retroactive Sentence Reductions: The 2007 Crack Cocaine Amendment" (May 2014), U.S. Sentencing Commission, http://www.ussc.gov/sites/default/files/pdf/research-and-publications/research-projects-and-surveys/miscellaneous/ 20140527_Recidivism_2007_Crack_Cocaine_Amendment.pdf.

> *"When stated in absolute numbers rather than rates, the growth in the size of the penal population has been extraordinary: in 2012, the total of 2.23 million people held in US prisons and jails was nearly seven times the number in 1972."*

The Incarceration Rate Has Been on a Steady Increase for Decades

National Academy of Sciences

In the following excerpted viewpoint, the National Academy of Sciences examines the expansion of incarceration in the United States. The authors begin by tracing trends in American imprisonment rates through the twentieth century and by comparing rates of incarceration in the United States with those in other countries. They then explore the fundamental question of the relationship of the growth in incarceration to crime. The empirical portrait presented in this viewpoint points strongly to the role of changes in criminal justice policy in the emergence of historically and comparatively unprecedented levels of penal confinement. The National Academy of Sciences is a private, nonprofit organization of the country's leading researchers that provides objective, science-based advice on critical issues affecting the nation.

Reprinted with permission from "Rising Incarceration Rates," by the National Academy of Sciences, Courtesy of the National Academies Press, Washington, DC.

As you read, consider the following questions:

1. How does the US incarceration rate compare internationally?
2. What does discussion and analysis of the US penal system generally focus on?
3. How have the rising numbers of parole violations contributed to the increase in incarceration rates?

In 1973, after 50 years of stability, the rate of incarceration in the United States began a sustained period of growth. In 1972, 161 US residents were incarcerated in prisons and jails per 100,000 population; by 2007, that rate had more than quintupled to a peak of 767 per 100,000. From its high point in 2009 and 2010, the population of state and federal prisoners declined slightly in 2011 and 2012. Still, the incarceration rate, including those in jail, was 707 per 100,000 in 2012, more than four times the rate in 1972. In absolute numbers, the prison and jail population had grown to 2.23 million people, yielding a rate of incarceration that was by far the highest in the world.[1]

[...]

The empirical portrait presented in this chapter points strongly to the role of changes in criminal justice policy in the emergence of historically and comparatively unprecedented levels of penal confinement. As a result of the lengthening of sentences and greatly expanded drug law enforcement and imprisonment for drug offenses, criminal defendants became more likely to be sentenced to prison and remained there significantly longer than in the past. The policy shifts that propelled the growth in incarceration had disproportionately large effects on African Americans and Latinos. Indeed, serving time in prison has become a normal life event among recent birth cohorts of African American men who have not completed high school.

US Incarceration in Historical and Comparative Perspective

The Bureau of Justice Statistics (BJS) has reported the incarceration rate for state and federal prisons from 1925 to 2012. Through the middle of the twentieth century, from 1925 to 1972, the combined state and federal imprisonment rate, excluding jails, fluctuated around 110 per 100,000 population, rising to a high of 137 in 1939. As noted earlier, after this period of relative stability, the imprisonment rate grew rapidly and continuously from 1972, increasing annually by 6 to 8 percent through 2000. The rate of growth slowed in the first decade of the 2000s, reaching a peak of 506 per 100,000 in 2007 and 2008. This high plateau was sustained through the end of the decade. In 2012, the imprisonment rate of 471 per 100,000 was still 4.3 times the historical average of 110 per 100,000. If the numbers in jail are added, the incarceration rate totaled 767 per 100,000 in 2007 and 707 per 100,000 in 2012 (Glaze and Herberman, 2013). When stated in absolute numbers rather than rates, the growth in the size of the penal population has been extraordinary: in 2012, the total of 2.23 million people held in US prisons and jails was nearly seven times the number in 1972.[2] The three levels of government together had expanded the nation's penal population by more than 1.9 million people since 1972.

The historically high US incarceration rate also is unsurpassed internationally. European statistics on incarceration are compiled by the Council of Europe, and international incarceration rates are recorded as well by the International Centre for Prison Studies (IPS) at the University of Essex in the United Kingdom. The 2011 IPS data show approximately 10.1 million people (including juveniles) incarcerated worldwide. In 2009, the United States (2.29 million) accounted for about 23 percent of the world total. In 2012, the US incarceration rate per 100,000 population was again the highest reported (707), significantly exceeding the next largest per capita rates of Rwanda (492) and Russia (474) (International Centre for Prison Studies, 2013). The Western European democracies have incarceration rates that, taken together, average around 100 per 100,000, one-seventh the rate of the United States. The former state socialist countries have very high incarceration rates by European standards, two to five times higher than the rates of Western Europe. But even the imprisonment rate for the Russian Federation is only about two-thirds that of the United States.

In short, the current US rate of incarceration is unprecedented by both historical and comparative standards.

Trends in Prison and Jail Populations

Discussion and analysis of the US penal system generally focus on three main institutions for adult penal confinement: state prisons, federal prisons, and local jails. State prisons are run by state departments of correction, holding sentenced inmates serving time for felony offenses, usually longer than a year. Federal prisons are run by the US Bureau of Prisons and hold prisoners who have been convicted of federal crimes and pretrial detainees. Local jails usually are county or municipal facilities that incarcerate defendants prior to trial, and also hold those serving short sentences, typically under a year.

This sketch captures only the broad outlines of a penal system with enormous heterogeneity. For example, several small states (Alaska, Connecticut, Delaware, Hawaii, Rhode Island, Vermont) hold all inmates (including those awaiting trial and those serving both short and long sentences) under the jurisdiction of a single state correctional agency. In Massachusetts, county houses of correction incarcerate those serving up to 3 years. Many prisons have separate units for pretrial populations. But this simple description does not encompass the nation's entire custodial population. Minors, under 18 years old, typically are held in separate facilities under the authority of juvenile justice agencies. Additional adults are held in police lockups, immigration detention facilities, and military prisons and under civil commitment to state mental hospitals.

Despite the great institutional complexity, prisons and jails account for the vast majority of penal confinement. It is here that the transformation of American criminal justice has been most striking, and it is here that the US incarceration rate increased to historically and internationally unprecedented levels.

Trends in the State Prison Population

State prisons accounted for around 57 percent of the total adult incarcerated population in 2012, confining mainly those serving time for felony convictions and parolees reincarcerated for violating their parole terms. Later in the chapter, we examine trends in state prison dynamics in greater detail, by offense categories, and decompose the effect of increased admission rates and increased time served on the rise in the rate of state imprisonment. The state prison population can be broadly divided into three offense categories: violent offenses (including murder, rape, and robbery), property offenses (primarily auto vehicle theft, burglary, and larceny/theft), and drug offenses (manufacturing, possession, and sale). In 2009, about 716,000 of 1.36 million state prison inmates had been convicted of violent crimes.

The most marked change in the composition of the state prison population involves the large increase in the number of those convicted for drug offenses. At the beginning of the prison expansion, drug offenses accounted for a very small percentage of the state prison population. In 1996, 23 percent of state prisoners were convicted of drug offenses (Mumola and Beck, 1997, p. 9). By the end of 2010, 17.4 percent of state prisoners had been convicted of drug crimes (Carson and Sabol, 2012, Table 9).

Trends in the Federal Prison Population

Federal prisons incarcerate people sentenced for federal crimes, so the mix of offenses among their populations differs greatly from that of state prisons. The main categories of federal crimes involve robbery, fraud, drugs, weapons, and immigration. These five categories represented 88 percent of all sentenced federal inmates in 2010.[3]

Federal crimes are quite different from those discussed above for state prisons. Robbery entails primarily bank robbery involving federally insured institutions; fraud includes violations of statutes pertaining to lending/credit institutions, interstate wire/communications, forgery, embezzlement, and counterfeiting; drug offenses typically involve manufacturing, importation, export, distribution, or dispensing of controlled substances; weapons offenses concern the manufacturing, importation, possession, receipt, and licensing of firearms and cases involving a crime of violence or drug trafficking when committed with a deadly weapon; and immigration offenses include primarily unlawful entry and reentry, with a smaller fraction involving misuse of visas and transporting or harboring of illegal entrants (Bureau of Justice Statistics, 2012a).

In the first decade, 1972 to 1980, the state prison and jail populations each grew by about 60 percent. In the 1980s, the incarcerated population more than doubled in size across all three levels. By 1990, the incarcerated population had increased to more than four times its 1972 level. By 2000, state prison and jail populations were about six times higher than in 1972, and their growth through the 2000s slowed significantly. Beginning from a much smaller base, the federal prison population grew at a much faster rate than the state prison and local jail populations in the 1980s and 1990s. Even in the 2000s, when penal populations in state and local institutions had almost ceased to grow, the population of the federal system increased in size by more than 40 percent from 2001 to 2010.

Trends in the Jail Population

In 2012, one-third of the adult incarcerated population was housed in local jails. Jail is often the gateway to imprisonment. Jails serve local communities and hold those who have been arrested, have refused or been unable to pay bail, and are awaiting trial. They also hold those accused of misdemeanor offenses—often arrested for drug-related offenses or public disorder—and those sentenced to less than a year. John Irwin's (1970) study of jail describes its occupants as poor, undereducated, unemployed, socially detached, and disreputable. Because of their very low socioeconomic status, jail inhabitants, in Irwin's language, are "the rabble," and others have similarly described them as "social trash," "dregs," and "riff raff" (Irwin, 1970, pp. 2–3; see also Cornelius, 2012).

The jail population is about one-half the size of the combined state and federal prison population and since the early 1970s has grown about as rapidly as the state prison population. It is concentrated in a relatively small number of large urban counties. The short sentences and pretrial detention of the jail population create a high turnover and vast numbers of admissions. BJS estimates that in 2012, the jail population totaled around 745,000, with about 60 percent of that population turning over each week (Minton, 2013, Table 7; Glaze and Herberman, 2013). In 2010, the nation's jails admitted around 13 million inmates (Minton, 2011). With such high turnover, the growth of the jail population has greatly expanded the footprint of penal confinement.

The Increasing Scope of Correctional Supervision

The significant increase in the number of people behind bars since 1972 occurred in parallel with the expansion of community corrections. Correctional supervision encompasses prisons and jails and also the community supervision of those on probation and parole. Probation usually supervises people in the community who can, following revocation for breach of conditions, be resentenced to prison or jail. Like the incarcerated population, the probation population increased greatly in absolute terms, from 923,000 in 1976 to 4.06 million in 2010, declining slightly to 3.94 million in 2012. Parole agencies typically supervise people who have served part of their sentence in prison and have been released back to the community, subject to such conditions as reporting to a parole officer, staying drug-free, and maintaining employment. Therefore, parole supervision can be expected to increase as its source, the numbers in prison, grows. From 1975 (the earliest year for which data are available) to 2010, the population under parole supervision grew by a factor of six, from 143,000 to 841,000. In 2012, it stood at 851,000.

The large probation and parole populations also expand a significant point of entry into incarceration. If probationers or parolees violate the conditions of their supervision, they risk revocation and subsequent incarceration. In recent decades, an increasing proportion of all state prison admissions have been due to parole violations (Petersilia, 2003, pp. 148ff). As a proportion of all state prison admissions, returning parolees made up about 20 percent in 1980, rising to 30 percent by 1991 and remaining between 30 and 40 percent until 2010. This represents a significant shift in the way the criminal justice system handled criminal offenses, increasing reliance on imprisonment rather than other forms of punishment, supervision, or reintegration. Parole may be revoked for committing a new crime or for violating the conditions of supervision without any new criminal conduct ("technical violators"), or someone on parole may be charged with a new crime and receive a new sentence.

The rising numbers of parole violations contributed to the increase in incarceration rates. The number of parole violators admitted to state prison following new convictions and sentences has remained relatively constant since the early 1990s. The number of technical violators more than doubled from 1990 to 2000. In 2010, the approximately 130,000 people reincarcerated after parole had been revoked for technical violations accounted for about 20 percent of state admissions (Carson and Sabol, 2012, Table 12; Glaze and Bonczar, 2011, Table 7). These returns accounted for 23 percent of all exits from parole that year (Glaze and Bonczar, 2011, Table 7).

The overall correctional population—including probationers and parolees—has grown substantially since 1972. By 2010, slightly more than 7 million US residents, 1 of every 33 adults, were incarcerated in prison or jail or were being supervised on parole or probation. At the end of 2012, the total was 6.94 million, or 1 of every 35 adults. The rise in incarceration rates should thus

MANDATORY MINIMUMS AND GUNS

The state Senate will soon vote on a bill that establishes a mandatory minimum sentence of up to eight years for felons who commit a crime using a gun.

The bill passed on a voice vote in the Assembly this week, but it's likely to face opposition in the Senate. Both Republican and Democratic backers of the bill say the law will help keep gun-toting criminals off the streets. But opponents like Milwaukee Democratic Sen. Lena Taylor say research shows mandatory minimums aren't effective in deterring crime.

Taylor said she's worried the law will fall the hardest on African-American men and increase racial disparity in the state's prisons.

"We lead in the nation in incarceration of African-American men per capita so we don't need more of the same. We need innovation," she said.

Taylor also expressed concern that because the bill eliminates judicial discretion, it will prevent judges from making an informed decision about which offenders really deserve a longer sentence and which might benefit from a shorter period behind bars.

The law would sunset in five years allowing lawmakers to assess whether it really has reduced gun crimes. Nicole Porter of the Washington, DC-based sentencing project said policymakers shouldn't count on it.

"What is effective in deterrence is the certainty of arrest or being held accountable, not necessarily severe or excessive prison terms," said Porter. "Lawmakers may think it makes sense that lengthening prison terms will serve as a deterrent effect. We know that in practice that's just not a pragmatic view."

Still, one of the bill's co-authors, Milwaukee Democratic Sen. Latonya Johnson, said she's convinced it's needed to protect public safety. She said it won't result in increasing the prison population.

"We want to balance not unnecessarily sending people to prison with making sure that our streets are safe," said Johnson.

Another Milwaukee Democrat, Sen. Evan Goyke, argued that a better long-term approach would be for the state to invest in community organizing efforts in the neighborhoods where gun crime is most prevalent.

"Investing in communities plagued by gun violence," said Goyke, "is much more effective at deterring and reducing crime than any kind of incarceration that you can do."

"Bill Increasing Mandatory Gun Crime Sentences Has Mixed Reception Among Dems," by Gilman Halsted, Wisconsin Public Radio, June 11, 2015.

be understood as just part of a broad expansion of the criminal justice system into the lives of the US population.

Variation in Incarceration Rates Among States

Trends in incarceration rates vary greatly among states. While the national imprisonment rate increased nearly 5-fold from 1972 to 2010, state incarceration rates in Maine and Massachusetts slightly more than doubled. At the other end of the spectrum, the rates in Louisiana and Mississippi increased more than 6-fold.

To see the change in trends, it is useful to divide the period since 1972 into two parts: from 1972 to 2000 and from 2000 to 2010. As discussed above, the period from 1972 to 2000 was a time of rapid growth for state prison populations; the change in incarceration rates in this period is indicated for each state in blue. The largest increases in this period generally occurred in southern and western states. From 1972 to 2000, incarceration rates grew most in Louisiana, Mississippi, Oklahoma, and Texas. In Louisiana, the rate grew by 700 per 100,000 population—more than 10-fold—rising to 801 per 100,000 by 2000, then climbing further to 867 by 2010. Growth in state incarceration rates was much slower in the northeast and midwest. In Maine and Minnesota, the rates grew by only around 100 per 100,000. These two states had the lowest incarceration rates by 2010—148 for Maine and 185 for Minnesota. In the period since 2000, incarceration rates have grown more slowly across the country. A few states have registered very large declines, including Delaware, Georgia, and Texas in the south and New Jersey and New York in the northeast.

The growth in the incarcerated population represents a broad transformation of penal institutions extending across the federal, state, and local levels and all regions of the country. Incarceration rates grew most from 1972 to 2000 and in the south and the west. Some evidence indicates a new dynamic emerging over the last decade, as growth in state incarceration rates has slowed significantly across the nation.

[...]

Endnotes

1. Small differences in incarceration rates from different sources result mainly from whether jurisdiction counts (prisoners under the jurisdiction of the state, a small number of whom may be housed in county facilities) or custody counts (the actual number housed in state facilities) are used. Only jurisdiction counts are available in a continuous series from 1925 to 2012. A total incarceration rate that includes the jail population should be based on custody counts; otherwise some double counting will occur whereby prisoners housed in county jails are also counted as being under state jurisdiction.

2. Here "incarceration" is used to refer to the numbers in prison or in jail at a given time. Consistent with the committee's charge and main focus on those sentenced to prison, generally for periods of a year or more, the term "incarceration" is used in much of the report to refer only to those in prison. However, where jails are discussed or the context does not make the usage clear, the terms "prison" and "jail" are used.

3. At least one-half of the remainder comprised those sentenced for possession/trafficking in obscene materials (3.7 percent) or for racketeering/extortion (2.7 percent) (Bureau of Justice Statistics, n.d.-b).

> *"Isn't it our moral obligation to protect the most vulnerable members of our society? If we don't, what does it say about us as a country? The rights of the victims, and the protection thereof, outweigh any perceived infringement of the rights of the criminals."*

Mandatory Sex Offender Registration Helps Keep Our Children Safer

The Daily News

In the following viewpoint, the editorial board of The Daily News *argues that sexual abuse and sexual assault are more common than anyone wants to believe. According to the Centers for Disease Control and Prevention, one in six boys and one in four girls are sexually abused before the age of eighteen. Therefore, it is essential to keep those victims, as well as potential victims, safe. But some people are worried about the rights of the sex offenders and their families. As the authors write, the sex offender registry is an example of when rights—the right of the sex offender, the right of the victim and the right of society—collide. So whose right takes precedent? Isn't it our moral obligation to protect the most vulnerable members of our society?* The Daily News *is a newspaper in Washington State.*

"Sex Offender Registry Helps Keep Us Safe," *The Daily News*, March 24, 2016. Reprinted by permission.

As you read, consider the following questions:

1. What were some of the objections to *The Daily News* editorials?
2. What percent of sexual assaults go unreported to law enforcement, according to National Research Council estimates?
3. How is the sex offender registry an example of when rights collide?

Raising kids is more than just feeding and housing them. Editorials we've written are filled with examples of where we, as a society, have failed. Whether we are talking about how Erin Andrews was treated, sexual assault in our society, treating each other with respect or the sex offender registry, we believe all of these are tied together in the quest to raise good citizens. We also believe the sex offender registry helps keep our kids—and community—safe.

It seems some people don't like what we have to say. We received some backlash from our March 13 editorial about the sex offender registry. People complained that our opinions were flawed because they have facts that disprove our assertions. We stand by our opinions and ask that you, the reader, learn about these topics and form your own opinions.

We had some people who were outraged at our support of the sex offender registry. Is the registry process perfect? Probably not. There isn't much in life that is perfect. But what do we do to protect our children?

Sexual abuse and assault is more common than you want to believe. According to the Centers for Disease Control, one in six boys and one in four girls are sexually abused before the age of 18. Just as we said about raising kids with good manners, respect for others and without misogynist tendencies, we need to do a better job protecting them from predators. The registry is one of the tools available to do that.

Some are worried about the rights of the sex offenders and their families. But what about the rights of the victims and their families, the rights of our citizens or the rights of possibly future victims? Others have said the registry creates hatred and violence which is directed at the offenders. Believing in the registry does not make it O.K. to harass, attack or intimidate those on the registry. The behavior goes against all we've written about. All people should be treated with respect and common courtesy.

The sex offender registry is an example of when rights collide; the right of the sex offender, the right of the victim and the right of society. So whose right takes precedent? Isn't it our moral obligation to protect the most vulnerable members of our society? If we don't, what does it say about us as a country? The editorial board believes the rights of the victims, and the protection thereof, outweigh any perceived infringement of the rights of the criminals.

The very nature of sex crimes and the lack of reporting also creates flaws in the "facts" related to claims about recidivism rates. Sexual crimes are reported far less than other types of crimes. The National Research Council estimates 80 percent of sexual assaults go unreported to law enforcement. Rape, Abuse & Incest National Network (RAINN) reports that 68 percent of sexual assaults go unreported. The discrepancy in the numbers doesn't change the fact that sex crimes are not reported nearly enough.

Because these numbers very greatly, even the most conservative estimate still skews the statistics so greatly that it seems nearly impossible to draw any conclusions on recidivism. How can groups claim there is low recidivism if the majority of these crimes are not even reported?

The Department of Justice reports on their website that, "due to the frequency with which sex crimes are not reported to police, the disparity between the number of sex offenses reported and those solved by arrest, and the disproportionate attrition of certain sex offenses and sex offenders within the criminal justice system, researchers widely agree that observed recidivism rates are underestimates of the true re-offense rates of sex offenders."

Other complaints we received were that the registry doesn't do any good because a large percentage of these crimes involve family members. While it is true that most sexual offenses are committed by someone the victim knows, that doesn't alleviate the need, in our opinion for the registry.

Whether it's your neighbor, cousin or a stranger in another neighborhood, we believe that as in all things, knowledge is power.

Whether it's monitoring your children's computers, phones and apps, knowing where they are at all times, knowing who their friends are, educating them on what to do in situations where they are vulnerable and knowing who the sex offenders are in your neighborhood, we believe we all need to do better.

"*Initial data on sexual assault trends since the inception of Megan's Law in the late 1990's suggest that rates have not significantly decreased and that, in many states rates may even be increasing.*"

Registration Has Had Little Impact

Kelly K. Bonnar-Kidd

In the following excerpted viewpoint, Kelly K. Bonnar-Kidd argues that sexual violence is a significant public health problem in the United States. In an effort to decrease incidents of sexual assault, legislators have passed regulatory laws aimed at reducing recidivism among convicted sexual offenders. As a result, sex offenders living in the United States are bound by multiple policies, including registration, community notification, monitoring via a global positioning system, civil commitment, and residency, loitering, and internet restrictions. These policies have led to multiple collateral consequences, creating an ominous environment that inhibits successful reintegration and may contribute to an increasing risk for recidivism. In fact, evidence on the effectiveness of these laws suggests that they may not prevent recidivism or sexual violence and result in more harm than good. Kelly K. Bonnar-Kidd is a professor in the Community Health Education Department at the State University of New York, Potsdam.

"Sexual Offender Laws and Prevention of Sexual Violence or Recidivism," by Kelly K. Bonnar-Kidd, American Public Health Association, March 2010. Reprinted by permission.

As you read, consider the following questions:

1. When was Megan's Law implemented?
2. What were some of the issues surrounding the effectiveness of Megan's Law?
3. How have states attempted to manage fear or hysteria in the community about the recidivism risk posed by registered sex offenders?

Empirical research examining Megan's Law has generally indicated that community notification is not effective in preventing sexually based crimes[24,29,39–46] and may actually create a context wherein the risk of recidivism increases.[47] Barnowski,[48] in his study of recidivism among 8000 sex offenders in Washington, found that the 5-year recidivism rate among those released from prison in 1990 was 5% higher than the rate among those released in 1997, the year community notification laws were implemented. That study's results must be interpreted with caution because the reduction in recidivism for registered sex offenders mirrored a statewide trend in reduced recidivism for other types of crimes. Recidivism rates were declining prior to community notification laws, and after an 11-year downward trend, the recidivism rates of registered sex offenders in Washington began to increase in 1997, the year Megan's Law was implemented. More recently, effectiveness studies from New Jersey[44] and New York[24] concluded that Megan's Law has had no significant impact on rates of recidivism or sexual violence, suggesting that the costs of implementing such laws may outweigh the benefits.

Collateral Consequences

Issues surrounding the effectiveness of Megan's Law would be unimportant if the consequences had little impact. However, community notification has many collateral consequences for both community members and registered sex offenders. According to Levenson et al.,[26] it is likely that parents experience fear after notification of a neighborhood sex offender. This fear can lead to community-wide hysteria, which has occurred in many towns.

In June 2007, for example, members of a small, rural community in New York were notified that 2 registered sex offenders were residing in their neighborhood and reacted by posting signs warning that "Monsters Live Here"; they also initiated a protest using the media and contacted the registered sex offenders' landlord asking that they be evicted. One resident noted that

> since he explained to his daughters about the 'monsters' across the street, he has seen a look of fear and terror in their faces, and they sometimes refuse to sleep alone.[49](pB1)

Another resident published a letter to the editor online in North Country This Week (St. Lawrence County, New York) in response to her new registered sex offender neighbor. One part of the letter read

> I have slept approximately a combined 5 hours in the past 3 nights because I wake up in a panic and I need to get up and make sure that my children are okay.[50]

This hysteria and panic is a collateral consequence of community notification. These kinds of reactions have led to a proliferation of registered sex offender laws above and beyond community notification. Since 1996, some states have created "safety zones," or places where a registered sex offender cannot be; others are mandating lifetime global positioning system (GPS) monitoring. Still others have successfully passed laws banning registered sex offenders from wearing Halloween costumes or mandating them to be indoors with outdoor lights off on Halloween night. In Louisiana in 2008, Governor Bobby Jindal signed SB 144, a bill making chemical castration through administration of the hormone medroxyprogesterone mandatory for certain offenders. In other states, registered sex offenders are subject to civil commitment, have been banned from using the Internet, have "sex offender" imprinted on their driver's licenses or license plates, and have lost all parental rights. Many registered sex offenders now also face restrictions related to employment and loitering and, most widespread, restrictions in where they can live.

Residency Restrictions

Because community members often react with fear to the presence of a registered sex offender, the mentality labeled "NIMBY" (not in my backyard) has led to the evolution of laws restricting where registered sex offenders can live. As of August 2006, more than 20 states and hundreds of localities nationwide had passed residency restrictions, and many more were considering them.[51,52] Usually passed retroactively, residency laws restrict registered sex offenders from living within a certain number of feet from schools, day-care centers, and churches, and their passage has produced much controversy. In California, Proposition 83 (also known as Jessica's Law) was passed in 2007 to limit registered sex offenders from living within 2000 feet of a school or a park. As a result of this ordinance, approximately 2700 registered sex offenders were told to move, with many ending up homeless.[53]

In some cases, residency restrictions are so severe that they essentially banish a registered sex offender from living anywhere in the city. In Miami, Florida, for example, residency restrictions were so strict—2500 feet from schools, playgrounds, licensed day-care centers, and parks—that the only location registered sex offenders' probation officers would approve for housing was underneath the Julia Tuttle Causeway, a bridge connecting Miami Beach to Miami.[54]

These laws have intuitive appeal. Who would want a registered sex offender living near children? When communities successfully get them to move, community members' fear subsides, thus making them feel safe. But there are logical problems with residency restrictions that could result in communities having a false sense of security.

Residency restrictions could violate registered sex offenders' fundamental human and constitutional rights, for example. In most cases, the laws are being applied retroactively to those who have served their time, which is a likely violation of *ex post facto* application of new laws as well as rights against double jeopardy. A case in Tippecanoe County, Indiana, serves as an example. A nonrecidivating 56-year-old man convicted in 1988 of a sex crime petitioned the court to relieve him of his duty to abide by residency restrictions. He had lived in his home for 7 years, a home that he shared with his wife and children; in July 2007, he was forced to move because his home was within 1000 feet of a church, a violation of the new residency restrictions.[55] Although the case is being appealed, a judge ruled that because the registered sex offender's wife owns the house, the residency restriction did not violate his property rights[56] and that residency restrictions, being a regulatory measure, do not violate registered sex offenders' constitutional rights.

Residency restrictions were developed on the basis of the assumptions that (1) registered sex offenders are at a high risk for recidivism, (2) sexual crimes are committed by strangers who lurk in areas where children congregate in an attempt to stereotypically abduct them, (3) all registered sex offenders have committed crimes against children, and (4) children and families are protected from sexual crimes if a registered sex offender does not live in their neighborhood. I addressed the first 2 assumptions earlier; recidivism rates among registered sex offenders are generally low, and most sexually based crimes are committed by someone known to the victim. As reported by Levenson and Cotter[57](p170) in their study of registered sex offenders' perceptions of residency restrictions, "Most abuse happens in homes or with family or close friends, not at bus stops or schools." The third assumption is also a public perception or myth created by the media.

Individuals who are required to register as sex offenders are those who have committed crimes against not only children but adults as well. Although the list of registerable sex offenses varies by state, registered sex offenders are also classified as those who have, for instance, possessed child pornography, solicited prostitution, participated in exhibitionism, or engaged in indecent exposure (including urinating in public), voyeurism, or oral or anal sex. Juveniles who have had consensual sexual relations with another juvenile also frequently fall under this category. In the United States in 2001, for example, children and adolescents younger than 18 years were arrested at a higher rate than any other age group (e.g., 140.7 per 100 000 arrests among those aged 13 to 14 years versus 74.6 per 100 000 arrests among those aged 40 to 44 years).[58] Although in the media we hear most often about sexual crimes committed against children, these are not the only crimes that lead to designation as a registered sex offender.

Furthermore, as mentioned, residency restrictions may provide a false sense of security in communities where registered sex offenders do not live.[46] People residing in registered sex offender-free areas are not automatically protected against sexual abuse.[26] In fact, evidence suggests that residency restrictions do not affect rates of sexual assault and therefore are ineffective.

The Minnesota Department of Corrections examined the "sexual reoffense patterns of 224 recidivists released between 1990 and 2002 who were reincarcerated for a sex crime prior to 2006"[59] and concluded that not one of the new offenses would have been prevented if residency restrictions had been in place. This makes intuitive sense. Residency restrictions simply mandate where a registered sex offender can and cannot live. It is possible for those few who seek to reoffend to drive or walk to a location if their intent is to commit another sex offense. In fact, the Minnesota Department of Corrections report acknowledged that "when direct contact offenders look for a victim, they are more likely to go to an area relatively close to home (i.e., within 20 miles of their residence), but still far enough away (i.e., more than 1 mile) to decrease the chances of being recognized."[59]

Risk-Level Determinations and Validity

Many states have attempted to manage fear or hysteria by establishing procedures for determining and notifying the community about the recidivism risk posed by registered sex offenders. Typically, there are 3 risk levels, high, medium, and low, differentiated according to a registered sex offender's "dangerousness" or risk for committing another sex offense. Those who are classified as high risk have a high potential for recidivating, whereas those who are classified as low risk are not likely to recidivate. The outcome of a high-risk classification is severe and includes but is not limited to additional registration requirements, community notification, residency restrictions, GPS monitoring, and potential civil confinement. Determinations of risk level are usually made on the basis of the outcome of an actuarial assessment.

Many risk-level determination assessments are in use in the United States, including the STATIC-99 and the Rapid Risk Assessment for Sexual Offense Recidivism.[60] Unfortunately, rarely can one ever predict with 100% accuracy the future behavior of a registered sex offender, even when using these actuarial assessments. However, the chances of correctly predicting future behavior increase when the instruments are valid.

Although a thorough discussion of the psychometric properties of these tools is beyond the scope of this review, research indicates that the validity of the tools is questionable.[61-63] The 3 best tools in use today have only moderate levels of predictive validity (i.e., area under the curve values of 0.64–0.70),[64] which in the field of public health is generally acceptable. However, moderate validity (a 30%–36% likelihood of error) should not be acceptable for instruments designed to limit freedoms and impose additional regulatory restrictions against registered sex offenders. In light of this, one must question whether moderate validity is acceptable in these cases. For example, Barnowski, in his study examining the relationship between risk levels and recidivism among registered sex offenders in Washington, concluded that "[t]he notification levels determined by the [End of Sentence Review Committee] do not classify sex offenders into groups that accurately reflect their risk for reoffending."[62]

[…]

Endnotes

24. Sandler J, Freeman NJ, Socia KM. Does a watched pot boil? A time-series analysis of New York State's sex offender registration and notification law. *Psychol Public Policy Law* 2008;14(4):284-302

26. Levenson JS, Brannon YN, Fortney T, Baker J. Public perceptions about sex offenders and community protection studies. *Anal Soc Issues Public Policy* 2007;7(1):1-25

29. Walker JT, Maddan S, Vasquez BE, VanHouten AC, Ervin-McLarty G. The influence of sex offender registration and notification laws in the United States. Available at: http://www.reentry.net/library/attachment.86354. Accessed December 3, 2009

39. Adkins G, Huff D, Stageberg P. The Iowa sex offender registry and recidivism. Available at: http://www.state.ia.us/government/dhr/cjjp/images/pdf/01_pub/SexOffenderReport.pdf. Accessed December 3, 2009

40. Fitch K. Megan's Law: Does it protect children? An updated review of evidence on the impact of community notification as legislated for by Megan's Law in the United States. Available at: http://www.nspcc.org.uk/Inform/publications/Downloads/meganslaw2_wdf48102.pdf. Accessed December 3, 2009

41. Levenson JS, D'Amora DA. Social policies designed to prevent sexual violence. *Crim Justice Policy Rev* 2007;18(2):168–199

42. Schram DD, Malloy CD. Community notification: a study of offender characteristics and recidivism. *Criminal Justice Stud* 2006;2:193–208

43. Zevitz RG, Farkas AF. Sex offender community notification: assessing the impact in Wisconsin. Available at: http://www.ncjrs.gov/pdffiles1/nij/179992.pdf. Accessed December 3, 2009

44. Zgoba KM, Witt P, Dalessandro M. Megan's Law: assessing the practical and monetary efficacy. Available at: http://www.ncjrs.gov/pdffiles1/nij/grants/225370.pdf. Accessed December 9, 2009

45. Welchans S. Megan's Law: evaluations of sexual offender registries. *Crim Justice Policy Rev* 2005;16(2):123–140

46. Craun SW, Theriot MT. Misperceptions of sex offender perpetration: considering the impact of sex offender registration. Available at: http://jiv.sagepub.com/cgi/content/abstract/0886260508327706v1. Accessed December 3, 2009 [PubMed]

47. Wakefield H. The vilification of sex offenders: do laws targeting sex offenders increase recidivism and sexual violence? *J Sex Offender Civil Commitment Sci Law* 2006;1:141–149

48. Barnowski R.Sex offender sentencing in Washington State: has community notification reduced recidivism? Available at: http://www.wsipp.wa.gov/rptfiles/05-12-1202.pdf. Accessed December 3, 2009.

49. McGrath M. Neighbors irate over sex offenders. *Watertown Daily Times* July 13, 2007:B1

50. North Country This Week Letter to the editor. Available at: www.northcountrynow.com. Accessed December 3, 2009

51. Tofte S. Sex offender laws do more harm than good. Available at: http://hrw.org/reports/2007/us0907. Accessed December 3, 2009

52. Norman-Eady S. Sex offender residency restrictions. Available at: http://www.cga.ct.gov/2007/rpt/2007-R-0380.htm. Accessed December 3, 2009

53. California Attorney General Sex offenders, sexually violent predators: punishment, residency restrictions, and monitoring. Available at: http://www.sos.ca.gov/elections/vig_06/general_06/pdf/proposition_83/entire_prop83.pdf. Accessed December 3, 2009

54. Zarrella J, Oppmann P. Florida housing sex offenders under bridge. Available at: http://www.cnn.com/2007/LAW/04/05/bridge.sex.offenders/index.html. Accessed December 3, 2009

55. Voravong S. John Doe's attorney argues law should not be retroactive. Available at: http://www.jconline.com. Accessed December 3, 2009

56. Indiana American Civil Liberties Union Legal docket. Available at: http://www.aclu-in.org/subpage.asp?p=32. Accessed on December 3, 2009

57. Levenson JS, Cotter LP. The impact of sex offender residence restrictions: 1,000 feet from danger or one step from absurd? *Int J Offender Ther Comp Criminol* 2005;49(2):168–178 [PubMed]

58. Federal Bureau of Investigation Age specific arrest rates for sex offenses. Available at: http://www.fbi.gov. Accessed December 3, 2009

59. Minnesota Dept of Corrections Residential proximity and sex offender recidivism in Minnesota. Available at: http://www.doc.state.mn.us/publications/documents/04-07SexOffenderReport-Proximity.pdf. Accessed December 3, 2009

60. Bureau of Justice Assistance Sex offender risk assessments. Available at: http://www.ojp.usdoj.gov/BJA/evaluation/psi_sops/sops-tools.htm. Accessed December 3, 2009

61. Logan WA. A study in actuarial justice: sex offender classification practice and procedure. Available at: http://wings.buffalo.edu/law/bclc/bclrarticles/3(2)/logan.pdf. Accessed December 3, 2009

62. Barnowski R. Sex offender sentencing in Washington State: notification levels and recidivism. Available at: http://www.wsipp.wa.gov/rptfiles/05-12-1203.pdf. Accessed December 3, 2009

63. Hanson RK, Morton-Bourgon KE. The characteristics of persistent sexual offenders: a meta-analysis of recidivism studies. Available at: http://ps-sp.gc.ca/res/cor/rep/_fl/crp2007-01-en.pdf. Accessed December 3, 2009 [PubMed]

64. New York State Division of Probation and Correctional Services Sex offender populations, recidivism and actuarial assessment. Available at: http://dpca.state.ny.us/pdfs/somgmtbulletinmay2007.pdf. Accessed December 3, 2009

> *"Over 60% of the federal district court judges responding to the Sentencing Commission survey indicated they considered federal mandatory minimum sentences too high."*

Mandatory Minimum Sentences Lead to Three Strikes Laws

Charles Doyle

In the following excerpted viewpoint, Charles Doyle argues that federal mandatory minimum sentencing statutes limit the discretion of a sentencing court to impose a sentence that does not include a term of imprisonment or the death penalty. The author states that they have a long history and come in several varieties: the not-less-than, the flat sentence, and piggyback versions. Federal courts may refrain from imposing an otherwise required statutory mandatory minimum sentence when requested by the prosecution on the basis of substantial assistance toward the prosecution of others. First-time, low-level, nonviolent offenders may be able to avoid the mandatory minimums under the Controlled Substances Acts, if they are completely forthcoming. Charles Doyle is Acting Law Librarian of Congress at the US Library of Congress.

"Federal Mandatory Minimum Sentencing Statutes," by Charles Doyle, Congressional Research Service Careers, September 9, 2013.

As you read, consider the following questions:

1. What do serious drug offenses for purposes of section 3559(c) consist of?
2. The federal three strikes provision recognizes convictions for two categories of serious violent felonies. What does the enumerated list consist of?
3. What does the more general, un-enumerated category consist of?

State and federal mandatory minimums have come under constitutional attack on several grounds over the years, and have generally survived. The Eighth Amendment's cruel and unusual punishments clause does bar mandatory capital punishment, and apparently bans any term of imprisonment that is grossly disproportionate to the seriousness of the crime for which it is imposed. The Supreme Court, however, has declined to overturn sentences imposed under the California three strikes law and challenged as cruel and unusual. Double jeopardy, *ex post facto*, due process, separation of powers, and equal protection challenges have been generally unavailing.

Three Strikes (18 U.S.C. 3559(c))

A defendant convicted of a federal "serious violent felony" must be sentenced to life imprisonment under the so-called three strikes law, 18 U.S.C. 3559(c), if he has two prior state or federal violent felony convictions or one such conviction and a serious drug offense conviction.[645]

Over 60% of the federal district court judges responding to the Sentencing Commission survey indicated they considered federal mandatory minimum sentences too high.[646] Although the survey asked specifically about sentences under other mandatory minimum statutes, it provided no opportunity for a response focused on section 3559(c).[647]

Notice and Objections

Section 3559(c) requires prosecutors to follow the notice provisions of 21 U.S.C. 851(a), if they elect to ask the court to sentence a defendant under the three strikes provision.[648] Section 851(a), in turn, requires prosecutors to notify the court and the defendant of the government's intention to seek the application of section 3559(c) and the description of the prior convictions upon which the government will rely.[649] Without such notice, the court may not impose an enhanced sentence.[650] The purpose of the requirement "is to ensure the defendant is aware before trial that he faces possible sentence enhancement as he assesses his legal options and to afford him a chance to contest allegations of prior convictions."[651] As long as that dual purpose is served, however, a want of meticulous compliance or complete accuracy will not preclude enhanced sentencing.[652] The objections most often raised are constitutional challenges and those that question the qualifications of prior convictions as predicate offenses.

Predicate Offenses

Serious Drug Offenses

Serious drug offenses for purposes of section 3559(c) consist of (a) federal drug kingpin offenses;[653] (b) the most severely punished of the federal drug trafficking offenses;[654] (c) the smuggling counterpart of the such trafficking offenses;[655] and (d) state equivalents of any of these three.[656] When the prosecution relies upon a state drug trafficking conviction, for example, it must show that the amount of drugs involved warranted treating it as an equivalent.[657]

Serious Violent Felonies

The federal three strikes provision recognizes convictions for two categories of serious violent felonies—one enumerated, the other general. The inventory of enumerated serious violent felonies consists of the federal or state crimes of:

- murder (as described in section 1111);
- manslaughter other than involuntary manslaughter (as described in section 1112);

A PLEA FOR REFORM

Research has shown that increasing time served does not help keep the public safe. Studies show that longer sentences have minimal or no benefit on future crime. Even worse, research shows a strong correlation between increased prison time and repeat offenses, meaning prison may create more serious and violent offenses when overused. For example, a 2002 study indicates that sentencing low-level drug offenders to prison may increase the likelihood they will commit crimes upon release. Research from the Arnold Foundation indicates that longer pretrial detention is associated with new criminal activity even after the case is resolved.

Law Enforcement Leaders members support reforming mandatory minimum laws. We urge Congress and state legislatures to reduce mandatory minimum sentences set by law, and also reduce maximum sentences. We will identify and speak out against unnecessarily harsh and counterproductive laws. Judges should be allowed more flexibility in sentencing and the discretion to determine appropriate punishments. With proportional sentences, we can reduce both sentence lengths and the likelihood individuals will commit further crimes.

Several states have done this while continuing to see crime fall to historic lows. New York State passed the "Rockefeller drug laws," imposing harsh mandatory sentences for drug possession in 1973. As a direct result, the state's prison population increased six-fold with striking racial disparities. In 2009, to slow the growth of its prison system, New York removed the law's mandatory minimums for low-level drug offenses, choosing instead to allow judges to use their discretion to determine appropriate sentence lengths or decide to send someone to treatment instead. Since 2009, the number of people sent to prison and the length of sentences has declined statewide. Sentencing disparities between minority and white defendants also narrowed by one-third. Now, those sent into treatment have only a 36 percent chance of committing a repeat offense, versus 54 percent for those incarcerated before the new law went into effect.

"Reforming Mandatory Minimums," Law Enforcement Leaders.

- assault with intent to commit murder (as described in section 113(a));
- assault with intent to commit rape; aggravated sexual abuse and sexual abuse (as described in sections 2241 and 2242);
- abusive sexual contact (as described in sections 2244(a)(1) and (a)(2);
- kidnapping;[658]
- aircraft piracy (as described in section 46502 of Title 49); - robbery (as described in section 2111, 2113, or 2118);
- carjacking (as described in 2119);
- extortion;[659]
- arson;[660]
- firearms use;[661]
- firearms possession (as described in section 924(c)); or
- attempt, conspiracy, or solicitation to commit any of the above offenses.[662]

The more general, unenumerated category consists of "any other [state or federal] offense punishable by a maximum term of imprisonment of 10 years or more that has as an element the use, attempted use, or threatened use of physical force against the person of another or that, by its nature, involves a substantial risk that physical force against the person of another may be used in the course of committing the offense."[663]

There are statutory exceptions for both categories. Among the enumerated offenses, arson offenses do not qualify as predicate offenses, if the defendant can establish by clear and convincing evidence that he reasonably believed the offense posed no threat to human life and that it in fact did not.[664] Moreover, neither robbery, attempted robbery, conspiracy to commit robbery, nor solicitation to commit robbery qualify, if the defendant can establish by clear and convincing evidence that the offense involved neither the use nor threatened use of a dangerous weapon and that no one suffered serious bodily injury as a consequence of the crime.[665]

Among the unenumerated offenses, this same no-weapon, no-injury standard applies—those otherwise qualifying 10-

year felonies, marked by the use or threatened use of physical force against another, do not qualify as predicate offenses, if the defendant can establish by clear and convincing evidence that no weapon was used, and no injury sustained, in the course of the offense.[666]

The question of what constitutes a conviction for an unenumerated "serious violent felony" under §3559(c) seems to have proven as perplexing as what constitutes a "violent felony" conviction under the Armed Career Criminal Act (ACCA).[667] Recent Supreme Court construction of the term "violent felony" in the ACCA may provide clarification for future cases arising under section 3559(c).[668]

Constitutional Considerations

Defendants sentenced under §3559(c) have raised many of the same constitutional arguments asserted by defendants subject to other mandatory minimum sentences. Here too, their arguments have been largely unavailing. Almendarez-Torres blocks the contention that prior convictions must be noted in the indictment and proven to the jury beyond a reasonable doubt.[669] Defendants who claimed that §3559(c) has a disparate racial impact and therefore offends equal protection have been unable to show, as they must, that it was crafted for that purpose.[670] The Eighth Amendment's grossly disproportionate standard has proven too formidable for defendants sentenced under the section to overcome.[671] The courts remain to be convinced that the mandatory minimum features of the section pose any separation of powers impediments.[672] Defendants who invoke double jeopardy have been reminded that "the Supreme Court has long since determined that recidivist statutes do not violate double jeopardy because 'the enhanced punishment imposed for the later offense is not to be viewed as either a new jeopardy or additional penalty for the earlier crimes, but instead as a stiffened penalty for the latest crime, which is considered to be an aggravated offense because a repetitive one.'"[673] Much the same response has awaited those in §3559(c) cases who seek refuge in *ex post facto*, "the use of predicate felonies to enhance a defendant's sentence does not violate the *Ex Post Facto* Clause because such enhancements do not represent additional penalties for earlier crimes, but rather stiffen the penalty for the latest crime committed by the defendant."[674]

Endnotes

645 18 U.S.C. 3559(c).

646 United States Sentencing Commission, Results of Survey of United States District Judges: January 2010 through March 2010, Question 1. Mandatory Minimums (June 2010), available at http://www.ussc.gov/ Judge_Survey/2010/JudgeSurvey_201006.pdf.

647 Id. A majority found the statutory mandatory minimums appropriate for trafficking in heroin, powder cocaine and methamphetamine; for firearms offenses; for aggravated identity theft; for production and distribution of child pornography; and for other child exploitation offenses. On the other hand, a majority found them too high for trafficking in crack cocaine (76%) or marijuana (54%); or receipt of child pornography (71%). Id.

648 18 U.S.C. 3559(c)(4).

649 21 U.S.C. 851(a)(1)("No person who stands convicted of an offense under this part shall be sentenced to increased punishment by reason of one or more prior convictions, unless before trial, or before entry of a plea of guilty, the United States attorney files an information with the court (and serves a copy of such information on the person or counsel for the person) stating in writing the previous convictions to be relied upon..."). E.g., *United States v. Sanchez*, 586 F.3d 918, 929-30 (11th Cir. 2009)("Prior to trial, the Government notified the district court and Camejo, pursuant to 18 U.S.C. §851, that if Camejo was found guilty of Counts 3, 4, or 5, it would ask the court to impose a life sentence, pursuant to 18 U.S.C. §3559(c), because he previously had been convicted in Florida circuit court of what §3559(c)(1)(A) deemed a 'serious violent felony' and two 'serious drug offenses'").

650 *United States v. Hood*, 615 F.3d 1293, 1302 (10th Cir. 2010); *United States v. Baugham*, 613 F.3d 291, 294 (D.C. Cir. 2010); *United States v. Morales*, 560 F.3d 112, 113 (2d Cir. 2009).

651 *United States v. Baugham*, 613 F.3d at 294-95; *United States v. Lane*, 591 F.3d 921, 927 (7th Cir. 2010).

652 *United States v. Hood*, 615 F.3d at 1302 (noting the appropriateness of "harmless error analysis" rather than "hypertechnical approach"); *United States v. Baugham*, 613 F.3d at 295 ("Our caselaw also makes clear, however, that to comply with §851(a) the information need not be perfect with respect to every jot and tittle"); *United States v. Boudreau*, 564 F.3d 431, 437 (6th Cir. 2009)("Indeed, we have regularly held that actual notice satisfies the requirements of Section 851(a)").

653 21 U.S.C. 848.

654 21 U.S.C. 841(b)(1)(A).

655 21 U.S.C. 960(b)(1)(A).

656 18 U.S.C. 3559(c)(2)(H).

657 *United States v. Sanchez*, 586 F.3d 918, 930 (11th Cir. 2009)(parenthetical citations in the original)("A state drug offense qualifies as a 'serious drug offense' under §3559(c) only if the offense, if prosecuted in federal court, would have been punishable under [21 U.S.C. §841(b)(1)(A)] or [21 U.S.C. §960(b)(1)(A)].... [For example,] to qualify as a 'serious drug offense' under §3559(c)(2)(H)(ii), the drug offenses must have been punishable under 21 U.S.C. §841(b)(1)(A). Section 841(b)(1)(A), however, is limited only to offenses involving '5 kilograms or more' of cocaine or '50 grams or more' of cocaine base").

658 18 U.S.C. 3559(c)(2)(E)("the term 'kidnapping' means an offense that has as its elements the abduction, restraining, confining, or carrying away of another person by force or threat of force").

659 18 U.S.C. 3559(c)(2)(C)("the term 'extortion' means an offense that has as its elements the extraction of anything of value from another person by threatening or placing that person in fear of injury to any person or kidnapping of any person").

660 18 U.S.C. 3559(c)(2)(B)("the term 'arson' means an offense that has as its elements maliciously damaging or destroying any building, inhabited structure, vehicle, vessel, or real property by means of fire or an explosive").

661 18 U.S.C. 3559(c)(2)(D)("the term 'firearms use' means an offense that has as its elements those described in section 924(c) or 929(a), if the firearm was brandished, discharged, or otherwise used as a weapon and the crime of violence or drug trafficking crime during and relation to which the firearm was used was subject to prosecution in a court of the United States or a court of a State, or both").

662 18 U.S.C. 3559(c)(2)(F)(i).

663 18 U.S.C. 3559(c)(2)(F)(ii).

664 18 U.S.C. 3559(c)(3)(B).

665 18 U.S.C. 3559(c)(3)(A).

666 Id.

667 E.g., *United States v. Abraham*, 386 F.3d 1033, 1038 (11th Cir. 2004)(escape constitutes a serious violent felony for purposes of section 3559(c)); *United States v. Dobbs*, 449 F.3d 904, 913-14 (8th Cir. 2006)(burglary is not a serious violent felony for purposes of section 3559(c)); *United States v. Evans*, 478 F.3d 1332, 1342 (11th Cir. 2007) (conviction for an anthrax threat against a federal building is not a serious violent felony for purposes of section 3559(c)).

668 *United States v. Rose*, 587 F.3d 695, 703-704 (5th Cir. 2009)(noting that circuit precedent construing the term "violent felony" in ACCA may be instructive when construing the term "serious violent felony" in section 3559(c)). The ACCA defines the term "violent felony" to mean "any crime punishable by imprisonment for a term exceeding one year ... that—(i) has as an element the use, attempted use, or threatened use of physical force against the person of another; or (ii) is burglary, arson, or extortion, involves use of explosives, or otherwise involves conduct that presents a serious potential risk of physical injury to another," 18 U.S.C. 924(e)(2)(B).

669 *United States v. Gonzalez*, 682 F.3d 201, 204 (2d Cir. 2012); United States v. Snype, 441 F.3d 119, 148 (2d Cir. 2006)("Thus, Almendarez-Torres continues to bind this court in its application of Apprendi.... With this understanding of the law, we identify no Sixth Amendment error in the district court's findings as to the fact of Snype's prior state robbery convictions. Four of our sister circuits have considered this question and reached the same conclusion"), citing *United States v. Cooper*, 375 F.3d 1041, 1053 n.3

(10th Cir. 2004); *United States v. Bradshaw*, 281 F.3d 278, 294 (1st Cir. 2002); United *States v. Weaver*, 267 F.3d 231, 251 (3d Cir. 2001); *United States v. Davis*, 260 F.3d 965, 969 (8th Cir. 2001).

670 *United States v. Washington*, 109 F.3d 335, 338 (7th Cir. 1997); *United States v. Farmer*, 73 F.3d 836, 841 (8th Cir. 1996). Equally unsuccessful was a defendant who claimed an equal protection violation based on disparate sentencing patterns from one state to another, *United States v. Wicks*, 132 F.3d 383, 389 (7th Cir. 1997)("Certain felonies— those described in (F)(i)—it [(Congress)] considered serious enough to include no matter how Draconian or lenient their treatment may be under state law, while others—those described in (F)(ii)—are subject to a congressional leveler through the requirement of the ten-year term of imprisonment. There is no federalism or equal protection issue at all in (F)(i), and none that survives rational basis analysis in (F) (ii)").

671 *United States v. Rose*, 587 F.3d at 704-705; *United States v. Gurule*, 461 F.3d 1238, 1247 (10th Cir. 2006); *United States v. Snype*, 441 F.3d 119, 152 (2d Cir. 2006); *United States v. Kaluna*, 192 F.3d 1188, 1199-200 (9th Cir. 1999); *United States v. DeLuca*, 137 F.3d 24, 40 n.19 (1st Cir. 1998); *United States v. Washington*, 109 F.3d 335, 337-38 (7th Cir. 1997); *United States v. Farmer*, 73 F.3d 836, 840 (8th Cir. 1996).

672 *United States v. Gonzalez*, 682 F.3d at 203; *United States v. Gurule*, 461 F.3d at 1246("As for the Three Strikes statute in particular, the few reported decisions of which we are aware from other circuits are unanimous in rejecting this [separation of powers] argument.... We agree with these precedents"), citing *United States v. Kaluna*, 192 F.3d 1188, 1199 (9th Cir. 1999); *United States v. Rasco*, 123 F.3d 222, 226-27 (5th Cir. 1997); *United States v. Washington*, 109 F.3d 335, 338 (7th Cir. 1997).

673 *United States v. Kaluna*, 192 F.3d at 1198-199, quoting *Witte v. United States*, 515 U.S. 389, 400 (1995) and *Gryger v. Burke*, 334 U.S. 728, 732 (1948); see also *United States v. Washington*, 109 F.3d at 338; *United States v. Farmer*, 73 F.3d 836, 840 (8th Cir. 1996).

674 *United States v. Abraham*, 386 F.3d 1033, 1038 (11th Cir. 2004); *United States v. Kaluna*, 192 F.3d at 1199; *United States v. Rasco*, 123 F.3d 222, 227 (5th Cir. 1997); *United States v. Washington*, 109 F.3d at 338; *United States v. Farmer*, 73 F.3d at 840-41.

Periodical and Internet Sources Bibliography

The following articles have been selected to supplement the diverse views presented in this chapter.

Albert W. Dzur, "Restorative Justice and Democracy: Fostering Public Accountability for Criminal Justice," *Contemporary Justice Review*, Vol. 14, No. 4, December 2011, 367–381.

Ryan Gentzler, "What's driving Oklahoma's prison population growth?" Oklahoma Policy Institute, February 9, 2016. https:// okpolicy.org/whats-driving-prison-population-growth/.

"In Final Act As President, Obama Commutes 330 Drug Sentences," *Chicago Tribune*, February 26, 2018. http://www.chicagotribune .com/news/nationworld/politics/ct-obama-commutes-drug-sentences-20170119-story.html.

Tom Lisi, "Darion Evans first Macon County juvenile cased affected by 2015 reforms," Herald & Review (Decatur, IL). September 22, 2017. http://herald-review.com/news/local/crime-and-courts/ darion-evans-first-macon-county-juvenile-cased-affected-by-reforms/article_732d27a0-a458-51b2-a136-5b8b29a14047.html.

Eric Luna, "Mandatory Minimums," Academy for Justice, October 7, 2017. http://academyforjustice.org/wp-content/ uploads/2017/10/7_Criminal_Justice_Reform_Vol_4_ Mandatory-Minimums.pdf.

James Q. Lynch, "Iowa House Approved Tougher Domestic Violence Penalties," The Gazette (Cedar Rapids, IA), March 9, 2016. http:// www.thegazette.com/subject/news/government/iowa-house-approved-tougher-domestic-violence-penalties-20160308

Matthew R. Segal, "A Clarifying Debate on Mandatory Minimums," *Massachusetts Lawyers Weekly*, June 17, 2015.

"Sex Offenders Who Fail to Register May Receive Life Sentence Under California's 'Three Strikes' Law," Prison Legal News, February 26, 2018. https://www.prisonlegalnews.org/news/2013/ oct/15/sex-offenders-who-fail-to-register-may-receive-life-sentence-under-californias-three-strikes-law/.

Mortimer B. Zuckerman, "Why We Should Get a Little Less Tough on Crime," *U.S. News Digital Weekly*, April 25, 2014, Vol. 6, Issue 17.

For Further Discussion

Chapter 1

1. Do you think mandatory minimum sentences are fair and just or harsh and ineffective? Why?
2. What has been the reality of mandatory minimum sentences as compared to their original intention?

Chapter 2

1. Which branch of the US government should determine mandatory minimum sentences? Provide specific evidence to back up your choice.
2. If "crime is crime," do you think that every guilty individual should receive the same mandatory minimum sentence? Why or why not?

Chapter 3

1. Do you think mandatory minimum sentences achieve equality, or do they discriminate against ethnic and racial minorities?
2. Do you think the Justice Safety Valve Act of 2013 is too limited in its scope? Why or why not?

Chapter 4

1. Do mandatory minimum sentences discourage from committing crimes, or do they have no effect on deterrence? Explain your answer with evidence from the viewpoints you've read.
2. Do you think Three Strikes laws help ensure that repeat offenders stay off the streets, or do they hurt the wrong people? Explain your reasoning.

Organizations to Contact

The editors have compiled the following list of organizations concerned with the issues debated in this book. The descriptions are derived from materials provided by the organizations. All have publications or information available for interested readers. The list was compiled on the date of publication of the present volume; the information provided here may change. Be aware that many organizations take several weeks or longer to respond to inquiries, so allow as much time as possible.

American Civil Liberties Union (ACLU)

125 Broad Street
18th Floor
New York, NY 10004-2400
(888) 567-ACLU
email: aclu@aclu.org
website: www.aclu.org

The ACLU is a national organization that works to defend civil liberties in the United States. It publishes various materials on the Bill of Rights, as well as regular in-depth reports, the *Civil Liberties* newsletter, and a set of handbooks on individual rights.

Center for Alternate Sentencing and Employment Services (CASES)

346 Broadway, 8th Floor
New York, NY 10013
(212) 732-0076
email: info@cases.org
website: www.cases.org

CASES seeks to end the overuse of incarceration as a response to crime. It operates two alternative sentencing programs: The Court Employment Project, which provides intensive supervision and services for felony offenders, and the Community Services Sentencing Project, which works with repeat misdemeanor offenders. The center advocates in court for such offenders' admission into its programs.

Criminal Justice Policy Foundation (CJPF)

8730 Georgia Avenue, Suite 400
Silver Spring, MD 20910
(301) 589-6020
email: info@cjpf.org
website: www.cjpf.org

The CJFP educates the public about the impact of drug policy and the problems of policing on the criminal justice system. It disseminates information and advice to policy makers, criminal justice professionals, and the public through consultation, education programs, conferences, publications, and the news media.

Drug Policy Alliance Network (DPAN)

70 W. 36th Street, 16th floor
New York, NY 10018
(212) 613-8020
email: nyc@drugpolicy.org
website: www.drugpolicy.org

DPAN advocates policies that reduce the harms of both drug misuse and drug prohibition. It works to reform drug policies that result in the incarceration, disenfranchisement, and harming of millions of nonviolent people.

Families Against Mandatory Minimums (FAMM)

1612 K Street NW, Suite 700
Washington, DC 20006
(202) 822-6700
email: famm@famm.org
website: www.famm.org

FAMM is an educational organization working to repeal mandatory minimum sentences in the United States. It provides legislators, the public, and the media with information on and analysis of minimum sentencing laws. FAMM publishes quarterly the newsletter *Famm-Gramm.*

Justice Policy Institute (JPI)

1012 Fourteenth Street NW, Suite 400
Washington, DC 10005
(202) 558-7974
email: info@justicepolicy.org
website: www.justicepolicy.org

The JPI advocates for sentencing reform and fair alternatives to incarceration through accessible research, public education, and communications advocacy. JPI strives to alleviate the US reliance on harsh sentencing policy.

National Association of Drug Court Professionals

4900 Seminary Road
Alexandria, VA 22310
(703) 575-9400
website: www.nadcp.org

Comprised of judges, prosecutors, defense attorneys, and clinical professionals, the NADCP strives to promote the use of drug courts as an alternative to mandatory minimum sentencing for low-level, nonviolent drug offenders.

National Center of Policy Analysis (NCPA)

12770 Coit Road, Suite 800
Dallas, TX 75251-1339
(972) 386-6272
email: publications@ncpa.org
website: www.ncpa.org

A nonprofit public policy research institute, NCPA addresses a range of issues. In dealing with crime, it advocates more stringent prison sentences, the abolishment of parole, and restitution for crimes.

National Criminal Justice Reference Service (NCJRS)

United States Department of Justice
Rockville, MD 20849-6000
(800) 851-3420
website: www.ncjrs.org

The NCJRS is one of the most extensive sources of information on criminal justice in the world. Its website provides topical searches and reading lists on many areas of criminal justice. Numerous publications on the justice system, drugs, crime, and other topics are available through its website.

National Prison Project

915 Fifteenth Street NW, 7th Floor
Washington, DC 20005
(202) 393-4930
email: mtartaglia@npp-aclu.org
website: www.aclu.org/prison

Formed in 1972 by the ACLU, this project serves as a national resource center and litigates cases to strengthen and protect adult and juvenile offenders' Eighth Amendment rights.

The Sentencing Project

514 Tenth Street NW, Suite 1000
Washington, DC 20004202-628-0871
email: staff@sentencingproject.org
website: www.sentencingproject.org

This organization seeks to provide public defenders, other public officials, and the public with information on establishing and improving alternative sentencing programs that provide convicted persons with positive and constructive options to incarceration.

United States Sentencing Commission (USSC)

One Columbus Circle NE, Suite 2-500, Sought Lobby
Washington, DC 20002-8002
(202) 502-4500
website: www.ussc.gov

The USSC is a bipartisan, independent agency located in the judicial branch of government, created by Congress in 1984 to reduce sentencing disparities and promote transparency and proportionality in sentencing. The commission collects, analyses, and distributes a broad array of information on federal sentencing practices.

Bibliography of Books

Rebecca Aldridge. *Mass Incarceration.* New York, NY: Greenhaven Publishing, 2018.

Cyndi Banks. *Criminal Justice Ethics: Theory and Practice.* Thousand Oaks, CA: Sage Publications, 2013.

Thomas G. Bloomberg (Editor, with others). *Advancing Criminology and Criminal Justice Policy.* New York, NY: Routledge, Taylor, and Francis Group, 2016.

William J. Chambliss. *Key Issues in Crime and Punishment.* Thousand Oaks, CA: Sage Publications, 2011.

United States Congress, United States Senate, Committee on the Judiciary. *Reevaluating the Effectiveness of Federal Mandatory Minimum Sentences.* Washington, DC: CreateSpace Publishing, 2017.

Michael J. Davis and Abigail M. White (Editors). *Federal Mandatory Minimum Sentencing: Sexual Offenses and Aggravated Identity Theft.* Hauppauge, NY: Nova Science Publishers, Inc., 2012.

Joe Domanick. *Cruel Justice: Three Strikes and the Politics of Crime in America's Golden State.* Berkley and Los Angeles, CA: University of California Press, 2004.

Charles Doyle. *Federal Mandatory Minimum Sentencing Statutes.* Library of Congress Congressional Research Service, Washington, DC: Penny Hill Press, 2013.

Charles Doyle. *Mandatory Minimum Sentencing Legislation in the 113th Congress.* Library of Congress Congressional Research Service: Washington, DC: CreateSpace Publishing, 2015.

Natalie Faulk. *The Downfall of America's Corrections: How Privatization, Mandatory Minimum Sentencing, and the Abandonment of Rehabilitation have Perverted the System Beyond Repair.* CreateSpace Publishing, 2016.

Raymond Goldberg. *Drugs Across the Spectrum.* United States: Wadsworth, 2014.

Renny Golden. *War on the Family: Mothers in Prison and the Families They Leave Behind.* New York, NY: Taylor & Francis, 2005.

Craig Hemmens (Editor). *Current Legal Issues in Criminal Justice.* New York, NY: Oxford University Press, 2007.

Stuart A. Kallen (Editor). *Legalizing Drugs.* Farmington Hills, MI: Greenhaven Press, 2006.

John Kroger. *Convictions: A Prosecutor's Battles against Mafia Killers, Drug Kingpins, and Enron Thieves.* New York, NY: Farrar, Straus, and Giroux, 2008.

Jack Lasky (Editor). *America's Prisons.* Farmington Hills, MI: Greenhaven Press, 2016.

Michael D. Lyman and Gary W. Potter. *Drugs in Society: Causes, Concepts, and Control.* Newark, NJ: LexisNexis Mathew Bender, 2007.

Mitchell B. Mackinem and Paul Higgins. *Drug Court: Construct the Moral Identity of Drug Offenders.* Springfield, IL: C.C. Thomas, 2008.

Liz Marie Marciniak. *Sentencing and Modern Reform: The Process of Punishment.* Durham, NC: Carolina Academic Press, 2016.

Doris Marie Provine. *Unequal Under the Law: Race in the War on Drugs.* Chicago, IL: University of Chicago Press, 2007.

Wade Riordan Raaflaub. *Mandatory Minimum Sentences.* Ottawa, Canada: Library of Parliament, 2006.

Paul Rand. *Taking a Stand: Moving Beyond Partisan Politics to Unite America.* New York, NY: Center Street, 2015.

Christophe Salaut (Editor). *Federal Mandatory Minimum Sentencing: Elements, Considerations, and Statutes.* Hauppauge, NY: Nova Science Publishers, Inc., 2013.

Frank Schmalleger and John Ortiz Smykla. *Corrections in the 21st Century.* Boston, MA: McGraw-Hill, 2007.

Courtney Semisch. *Alternative Sentencing in the Federal Criminal Justice System.* Washington, DC: United States Sentencing Committee, 2009.

Samual Walker, Cassia Spohn, and Miriam Delone. *The Color of Justice: Race, Ethnicity, and Crime in America.* Belmont, CA: Wadsworth Publishing, 2012.

Index